A Practical Guide to
Phonics

Gotham Books

30 N Gould St.
Ste. 20820, Sheridan, WY 82801
https://gothambooksinc.com/

Phone: 1 (307) 464-7800

© 2025 *Beverly Blount*. All rights reserved.

No part of this book may be reproduced, stored in a retrieval system, or transmitted by any means without the written permission of the author.

Published by Gotham Books (January 30, 2025)

ISBN: 979-8-3481-1168-7 (H)
ISBN: 979-8-3481-1165-6 (P)
ISBN: 979-8-3481-1166-3 (E)

Because of the dynamic nature of the Internet, any web addresses or links contained in this book may have changed since publication and may no longer be valid.

The views expressed in this work are solely those of the author and do not necessarily reflect the views of the publisher, and the publisher hereby disclaims any responsibility for them.

TABLE OF CONTENTS

FIRST PART | PAGE

ACKNOWLEDGEMENTS	xii
PREFACE	xiii
SOUNDS IN THE ENGLISH LANGUAGE	xiv
INSTRUCTION PAGES: STUDENTS AND TEACHERS	xvi
ENGLISH	xviii
SPANISH	xix
FRENCH	xx
PORTUGUESE	xxi
GERMAN	xxii
JAPANESE	xxiv
FIRST LEVEL: THREE LETTER PHONETIC WORDS	1
SECOND LEVEL: LONGER PHONETIC WORDS AND CONSONANT BLENDS	5
2ND AND 3RD GROUPS: READING TWO AND THREE WORD PHRASES	12
FOURTH GROUP: INTRODUCTION OF "A" AS A WORD IN ITSELF	15
FIFTH GROUP: ADJECTIVE PHRASES "THE"	16
SIXTH GROUP: PREPOSITION PHRASES	17
SENTENCES	18
SIMPLE RULES	20

SECOND PART
PAGE

SOUNDS AND SENTENCES	24
a_e = long ā_silent e	38
a #1 = ä	40
a #2 = long ä	42
a #3 = e	43
a #4 = i (y = ē)	43
a #5 = u	44
able = uble (silent e)	45
able = long ā + bul (silent e)	47
ace = long ā + s (silent e)	49
age #1 = long ā + j (silent e)	51
age #2 = ej (silent e)	53
ah = ä	55
ai = long ā	57
ain = en	59
air = âr	61
al #1 = aw	63
al #2 = awl	65
al #3 = ul	67
ang = long ā + nj	69
ant = unt	71
ar #1 = r	73
ar #2 = er	75
ar #3 = âr	77
are = âr	79
ation = long ā + shun	81
au = å	83
augh #1 = ä	85
augh #2 = af	86
aw = aw	87
ay = long a	89
be = b + long ē	91
ce #1 = s (silent e)	93
ce #2 = se	95
ce #3 = se + long e	97
ce #4 = sh	97
cean = shun	98
cei = s + long ē	98
ch #1 = ch	99
ch #2 = k	101
ci #1 = sh	103
ci #2 = si	106
ci #3 = s + long ī	108
cious = shus	109
cir = sr	110
co = cu	111
ct	112
cu = ceu	114
cy #1 = s + long ē	115
cy #2 = si	116
cy #3 = s + long ī	118
de = d + long ē	120
dge = j	122
di = d + long ī	124
e #1 = long ē	125
e #2 = short i	127
e #3 = silent e	128
e_e = long ē_e	130
ea #1 = long ē (silent a)	132
ea #2 = long ā	134
ea #3 = silent a	135
ea #4 = long ēā	138
ear #1 = long ē + r	139
ear #2 = âr	140
ear #3 = er	141
ear #4 = ar	142

eau = ea	142	i #1 = long ī	182
ed #1 = d	143	i #2 = long ē	184
ed #2 = id	145	i #3 = u	185
ed #3 = t	147	ice #1 = is	186
ee = long ē	149	ice #2 = long ī + sz	187
eer = long ē + r	151	ie #1 = long ē (silent i)	188
ei #1 = long ā	152	ie #2 = long ī (silent e)	190
ei #2 = long ē	153	i - e #3 = long ī_silent e	192
eigh = long ā	154	ier = long ē + r	194
eign #1 = in	155	ies #1 = long īz	195
eign #2 = long ā + n	155	ies #2 = ēz	196
eir #1 = long ē	156	igh = long ī	198
eir #2 = âr	156	ing = ing	200
el = ul	157	io = long īō	204
eo = long ē	158	ious = long ē + us	204
er #1 = r	159	ion = yun	205
er #2 = long ē + r	161	ir = r	206
ere #1 = long ē + r	161	ire = long ī + r	208
ere #2 = â + r	162	ise = long ī + z	210
es = z	162	jua = whä	210
eu = eu	163	kn = n (silent k)	211
eve = long ē + v	163	le = ul	212
(silent e) (rule ē _e)	163	mb = m (silent b)	215
ew = eu	164	mn = m (silent n)	216
ey #1 = long ē	165	ng = ng	217
ey #2 = ā	167	o #1 = long ō	218
eyre = âr + long ē	168	o #2 = ôô	220
ir + long ē	168	o #3 = u	222
g =j	169	o_e #1 = long ō_silent e	224
ge =j	171	o_e #2 = u_silent e	226
gi =ji	173	oa #1 = long ō	228
gn =gn (silent g)	175	oa #2 = ä	230
gth = silent g + th	176	oar = long ō + r	231
gue = g	177	oe = long ō	232
gy = ji	179	oi = oi	233
silent h	180	ol = long ō + l	235

on #1 = un	237	qu = kw	289
on #2 = won	239	qua = kwä; que = kwe	291
oo #1 = long ōō	242	re = r + long ē	293
oo #2 = ôô (book)	244	sc = s (silent c)	295
oo #3 = ōō/ôô	247	se = long vowel + z	296
oo #4 = u	248	sh = sh	298
oor = long ō + r	249	shion = shun	300
or #1 = or	250	sion = shun	300
or #2 = er	252	silent t = ŧ	302
ore = long ōr	254	ssion = shun	304
otion = long ō + shun	256	sure = shr	306
ou & oul #1 = ōō	257	tch = ch (silent t)	308
ou #2 = ow	258	th #1 = th	310
ou #3 = long ō	260	th #2 = th	312
ou #4 = u	260	th #3 = thu	
ough #1 = ō	262	(non-phonetic)	314
ough #2 = ou	262	tion = shun	316
ough #3 = ät	263	tune = chn	319
ough #4 = long ōō	265	ture #1 = chr	320
ough #5 = uf	265	tur/ture #2 = tyōōr	322
our #1 = our	266	u #1 = û	323
our #2 = long ō + r	267	u #2 = ü (ue)	325
our #3 = r	268	u #3 = long ū + silent e	327
ous = us	269	u #4 = silent u	329
ove = long ōō + v (silent e)	271	u_e = ü (silent e)	331
ow #1 = ow	272	ue #1 = ōō	333
ow #2 = long ō	275	ue #2 = eu	335
oy = oi	278	uge = euj	337
per = pr	280	ugh #1 = f	338
pn = n (silent p)	280	ugh #2 = eu	340
ph = f	281	ui #1 = ōō	341
pre = pr + long ē	283	ui #2 = long ī	342
pro #1 = prä	285	ur #1 = r	343
pro #2 = pr + long ō	286	ur #2 = er + long ē	345
ps = s (silent p y = ī)	288	ur #3 = uer	346
		ure = yōōr	347

use = long ū + z	349
uy = long ī	351
silent w	352
wa #1 = wä	353
wa #2 = wa	354
war = wr (name of r)	355
wh = wh	357
who = hōō	359
wo #1 = wû	360
wo #2 = wun	361
wor = wr	362
y #1 = long ē	363
y #2 = i	365
y #3 = long ī	367
yr = ur	369
yre = long ī +r	371
PUZZLE WORDS	372
SPANISH PRONUNCIATIONS	379
ABOUT THE AUTHOR	380
OTHER PUBLICATIONS AND AWARDS	382

I have been working for more than 20 years with Beverley as she developed her guide. We designed material to be used with the lists as she added words, phrases and more combinations of sounds. The material enabled the children to construct correctly their ongoing knowledge of reading and comprehension step by step. Although most of our children are non-native English speakers, they read with correct pronunciation and a very high level of English reading comprehension.

My daughter continued through Beverley's Elementary school and is now in England where she amazes people with her impressive pronunciation and reading of English. All of her friends that were together through our Kinder and Elementary school equally excel in reading and pronouncing English.

Claudia Capon, Director of the Christa McAuliffe Montessori School, Mexico City

Also by the author:

The Secret of the Haunted Hacienda
Lucifer
The Mystery of the Tarascan Ruins
The Monarch Mystery
10 Horses and a Pony
El Dorado
Love's End
Silversuit I and II
Silversuit III

Written under her pen name, B. Palma. Contact author at her web page and blog: www.paloalto-bilingual-adventures.com

To the hundreds of children who have used this system and are avid readers.

And to my lawyer Rafael López Ibarra who has been my steadfast supporter for so many years.

Matching Letters With Objects Beginning With That Letter

ACKNOWLEDGEMENTS

As this book was written over many years, it is impossible to list all those who helped me in one way or another, especially the teachers of my schools who used this work as it unfolded in their classrooms.

I can only say to those faces from the past, "Thank you."

Claudia Capon, Director of one of my Montessori schools supervised generations of teachers while I developed this system. My daughter, Beverley Argus Calvo Ph.D., helped and encouraged me at the very start and daughter Beth Argus, MA, MFT, has always been a dear supporter.

Patient Ana Luisa Pérez Chiñas repaginated it a thousand times.

PREFACE

This manual is designed to make it simple to teach readers from kindergarten through ninety to master the difficult-seeming task of reading, pronouncing and spelling a very complex language.

Beverley Blount M.Ed

SOUNDS IN THE ENGLISH LANGUAGE

Short Vowel Sound
- **a** as in ant
- **e** as in elf
- **i** as in it
- **o** as in on
- **u** as in up

Long Vowel Sounds
- **ā** as in April
- **ē** as in even
- **ī** as in I
- **ō** as in open
- **ū** as in unit

Consonant Diagraphs
- **sh** as in ship
- **wh** as in when
- **th** as in thin
- **ng** as in ring
- **ch** as in chip
- **th** as in this
- **kn** as in knee
- **qu** as in quit
- **ph** as in f
- **ñ** as in canyon

Consonant Sounds
- **b** as in bat
- **c** as in cat
- **d** as in dog
- **f** as in fat
- **g** as in gun
- **h** as in hat
- **j** as in jet
- **k** as in kit
- **l** as in leg
- **m** as in man
- **n** as in nest
- **p** as in pig
- **q** as in quit
- **r** as in run
- **s** as in sit
- **t** as in tan
- **v** as in van
- **w** as in wet
- **x** as in ax
- **y** as in yet
- **z** as in zip

Murmor Diphthongs
- **ar** as in car (R)
- **er** as in her (r)
- **ir** as in sir (r)
- **ôr** as in corn
- **ur** as in burn (r)

Vowel Combinations
- **oŏ** as in book
- **ōō** as in pool
- **oi** as in oil
- **eu** as in neuter
- **ou** as in out
- **aw** as in aw

Other Vowel Sounds
- **å** as in all
- **â** as in air
- **ä** as in across
- **ü** as in eu
- **û** as in oŏ

TEACHERS OF ENGLISH

You will find this simple guide a great help in improving your student's pronunciation of English. Be very careful yourself in sounding out the letters and forget the old ABC's you learned in school. From now on, think ah-bu-ku.

Have the students read aloud to you as much possible from the lists and dictate the sets of words using those sounds if possible.

The pronunciation guide can be given to any child or adult that can read any language at least passably. It can be a great addition to any English program. Because dictionaries do not always use phonetic words as examples of letter sounds. I have only used simple phonetic words in my guide and have reduced the number of sounds to a minimum.

学英语的学生

此为英语语言发音的简单指导会有助于掌握一门复杂语言的发音、朗读和拼读，这些看上去是件困难的任务。

整个学习的关键在于对第 xiii 页上所列举的发音的记忆和练习，为此你需要一个对基础英语发音正确的人的帮助。

然后你会继续靠自己或者跟有一个说英语的人的帮助。首先不要急于学习这单词的词义，它们是作为发音而非为上下文意思。

本书的几个部分划分如下：第 xiii 页列举了英语语言的基础发音，首先是短音节和基本辅音，列举的所有单词都使用这些音，除非另有所指。从 xiii 页到 xlvi 页列举了仅仅含有这些音的单词，当你掌握了这些列举的词，你就能继续掌握从第 1 页到第 357 页上按照字母顺序的列举的比较困难的发音。练习朗读这些发音词然后再读读练习多种变化的词。有一个说英语母语的人在旁帮助会更理想。

学生和教师

发音的组合按照字母顺序列举有助于查找对那些会迷惑你的音。记下所有列举的词汇丰富你的发音。第 359-367 页所列举的词 "puzzle word" 没有遵循什么规则，它们必须作为常见词学会，这些常见词我都使用正确发音代码写在每个音的旁边。

我已经发现把英语作为第二语言的我的学生们在发音方面的迅速进展。

我非常希望那些使用这种学习方法的人也会发现他们在正确地发音。

A Practical Guide to Phonics　　　　　　　　　　　　　　　　Page xvii

STUDENTS OF ENGLISH:

This simple guide to the sounds of the English language will help you master the difficult seeming task of pronouncing, reading and spelling a very complex language. The key to the entire program is the memorization and practice of the sounds given on page xiii. For this you need to have the aid of a person that speaks correctly basic American English. After that you may continue on your own or hopefully, have the continued aid of an English-speaking person. Don't worry about learning the meaning of the word first, they were chosen for their sounds not context. The sections of the book are divided as follows: page xiii has the lists of the basic sounds in the English language. The short vowel sound and the basic consonant sounds are given first. All words on the lists use these sounds unless otherwise indicated. On pages xxxi through xlvi, are lists of words that only contain these basic sounds. When you master these lists, you will be able to go on to more difficult sounds in the alphabetical lists on pages liii through 346. Practice reading the phonetic words before you go on to the many variations. The continued aid of a native English-speaking person would be ideal.

STUDENTS AND TEACHERS:

The combinations of sounds are listed in alphabetical order to facilitate looking up sounds that may puzzle you. Jot down words on the lists yourself to enrich your pronunciation. There are lists (pages 339-347) of words "puzzle words" that do not follow any rule. They must be learned as sight words using the sounds beside each one I used in coding the correct pronunciation. I have found that my ESL students show an immediate improvement in their pronunciation. My best wishes that all who use this program may also find themselves pronouncing English correctly.

Beverley Blount, M. Ed

MAESTRAS DE INGLES:

Ustedes encontrarán esta simple guía como una gran ayuda para mejorar la pronunciación en inglés de sus estudiantes. Sean muy cuidadosos al pronunciar las letras y olviden el viejo ABC que ustedes aprendieron. De ahora en adelante piensen en ah-bu-ku. Hagan que sus alumnos lean las listas en voz alta, lo mas que puedan y si es posible dictarles la serie de palabras. Este programa puede ser dado a cualquier niño o adulto que pueda leer lo básico en cualquier idioma. Puede ser un gran plus para cualquier programa de inglés.

ESTUDIANTES DE INGLES:

Esta sencilla guía de los sonidos del idioma inglés, les ayudará a dominar lo que parece difícil de pronunciar y deletrear.

La clave para este programa completo es la memorización y práctica de los sonidos dados en la página xiii. Para esto se necesita la ayuda de una persona que hable correctamente el idioma inglés. Después de eso pueden continuar solos, aunque sería mejor contar con la ayuda de una persona de habla inglesa. No se preocupen por aprender el significado de las palabras al principio; fueron escogidas por sus sonidos, no por su contexto.

Las secciones del libro se dividen como sigue: En la página xiii están los sonidos básicos de las vocales y los de las consonantes. Todas las palabras en las listas utilizan estos sonidos a menos que tengan alguna otra indicación.

De la página xxxi hasta la xlvi hay listas de palabras que sólo contienen estos sonidos básicos. Cuando domine estas listas, será capaz de pasar a los sonidos más difíciles de las listas alfabéticas que aparecen de la página liii a la 346. Practique leyendo las palabras fonéticas antes de continuar con las otras muchas variaciones. Si se tiene una persona de habla-inglesa a la cual le pueda leer en voz alta estas listas, sería mucho major.

ESTUDIANTES Y MAESTRAS:

La combinaison de sonidos está enlistada en orden alfabético para facilitar el buscar los sonidos que puedan confundirlos. Escriba las palabras para enriquecer su propio diccionario de pronunciación. Al final, encontrará una lista (páginas 339-347) de palabras, "puzzle words", las cuáles no siguen ninguna regla. Estas deberían aprenderse usando los sonidos, los cuales fueron escritos al lado de cada palabra. Yo he encontrado que mis alumnos han mostrado una mejoría inmediata en su pronunciación. Mis mejores deseos para que ustedes también logren hablar un correcto inglés.

ESTUDIANTS DE LANGUE ANGLAISE:

Ce simple guide des sons de la langue anglaise, vous aidera à dominer e qui vous semble difficile de prononcer et d'épeler.

Le secret de ce programme complet est la mémorisation et la pratique des sons donnés sur la page xiii. Pour cette raison, il est nécessaire l'aide d'une personne qui parle parfaitement la langue anglaise. Apres avoir appris les sons, vous pourrez continuer le programme seul mais il est préférable d'être suivi par cette personne de langue anglaise. Au début, ne vous inquiétez pas pour apprendre la signification des mots. Ils n'ont pas été choisis pour leur signification sinon pour leur son.

Le livre se divise de cette façon: Sur la page xiii se trouve les sons principaux de la langue anglaise. Premièrement, on donne les sons principaux des vocales, ensuite ceux des consonnes. Yous les mots employés sur cette liste, ont les sons principaux à moins d'une indication contraire. Sur les pages xxxi jusqu' xlvi y a les listes de mots qui contiennent uniquement les sons principaux.

Lorsque vous dominerez ces listes, vous pourrez penser aux sons plus difficiles des listes alphabétiques, qui se trouvent sur la page liii à la 346. Etudiez en lisant les mots phonétiques avant de continuer avec les autres variations. Si une personne de langue anglaise pouvait vous dicter les mots, le résultat serait beaucoup mieux.

ESTUDIANTS ET PROFESSEURS:

La combinaison des sons est listée dans l'ordre alphabétique pour faciliter la recherche des sons qui peuvent se confondre. Ecrivez les mots pour enrichir votre propre dictionnaire. A la fin vous trouverez une liste de mots pour faire votre propre examen. Chaque mot contient au moins deux sons différents. Organisez votre propre code. J'ai pu observer que mon étudiants ont améliore immédiatement leur prononciation avec ce programme. Mon meilleur souhait pour que vous puissiez parler la langue anglaise correctement.

ESTUDANTES DE INGLES:

Esta simples guia das pronunciações do idioma inglês vos ajudará a dominar o que parece tão difícil de pronunciar e soletrar.

A clave para este programa completo é a memorização a prática da pronunciação da transcrição da pronúncia da página xiii. Para isso se necessita a ajuda de uma pessoa que fale corretamente o idioma inglês depois disso você pode continuar sozinho.

Não se preocupe em aprender o significado das palavras, porque foram escolhidas por seus sons e não por seu contesto.

As partes do livro se dividem da seguinte maneira: Na página xiii estão as pronúncias básicas do idioma inglês. Primeiro damos a pronúncia básica das vogais e das consoantes. Todas as palavras que estão na lista utilizam estas pronúncias, sempre que não tenha alguma outra indicação.

Nas páginas xxxi e xlvi tem listas de palavras que contem as pronúncias básicas. Quando aprenda bem estas palavras, você será capaz de pronunciar as mais difíceis que aparecem nas páginas liii e 346.

É multo importante que você esteja bem familiarizado com as palavras fonéticas, praticando, antes de continuar, "se possível", com uma pessoa que domine a língua inglesa.

ESTUDANTES E PROFESSORES:

As combinações das pronúncias estão em ordem alfabética para facilitar a procura das palavras que possam causar confusão.

Escreva e leia palavras para praticar e enriquecer o seu vocabulário.

Ao final, há uma lista de palavras que você pode usar para praticar. Cada uma destas palavras tem dois tipos de pronunciação.

Meus melhores desejos para que vocês logrem um correto inglês.

ENGLISCHCHUELER:

Diese einfachen Richtlinien del Laute der englischen Sprache werden Ihnen helfen zu beherrschen, was so schwierig auszusprechen und zu buchstabieren scheint.

Der Schluessel zu diesem kompletten Programm ist das Einpraegen und die Uebung der auf der Buchseite xiii. Hierfuer braucht man die Hilfe einer Person, die die englische Sprache richting beherrscht. Danach kann man allein weitermachen, obwohl es besser waere, wenn eine englisch sprechende Person helfen koennte. Es ist anfangs nicht erforderlich, die Bedeutung der Woerter zu lernen; sie wurden nach ihren Lauten ausgesucht, nicht nach uhrer Bedeutung.

Die Abschnitte des Buches sind wie folgt aufgeteilt: Auf Seite ain finden Sie die Grundlaute der englischen Sprache.

Zuerst die Grundlaute der Vokale und der Konsonanten.

Alle Woerter dieser Liste gebrauchen diese Laute, es sei denn, etwas anderes ist angegeben. Auf den Seiten xxxi und xlvi sind Woerter aufgelister, die nur diese Grundlaute enthalten.

Wenn Sie diese Listen beherrschen, werden Sie in der Lage sein, zu den schwierigeren Lauten der alphabetischen Listen, die auf den Seiten liii bis 346 erscheinen, ueberzugehen.

Lesen Sie zuerst die phonetischen Woerter, bevor Sie mit den vielen anderen Variationen fortfahren. Falls es eine Person gibt, die englisch spritch und Ihnen diktirien koennte, waere dies wesentlich besser.

SCHUELER UND LEHRER:

Die Kombination von Lauten ist in alphabetischer Reihenfolge aufgeführt, um das Suchen der Laute, die Sie verwirren könnten, zu erleichtern.

Schreiben Sie Woerter, um Ihren persönlichen Aussprache Wortschatz zu erweitern. Am Ende gibt es eine Liste von Woerten, die Sie benutzen können, um sich zu prüfen. Jedes dieser Wörter hat mindestens verschiedene Laute. Finden Sie Ihren eigenen Code.

Meine Erfahrung ist, dass meine Schülers eine sofortige Verbesserung in ihrer Aussprache gezeigt haben.

Meine besten Wünsch, damit auch Sie ein korrektes Englisch sprechen.

英語を学ぶ生徒へ：

　　　　この簡単な英語の音声のガイドは、あなたも困難に思われがちな発音や解読をマスターするのに役立つことと思われます。

　　　　全プログラムのかぎは、最初のページに記された音声の暗記と練習にあります。これらは英語を正確に話す上で必要な助けとなります。それから後は、独自で学習を続けられます。（しかしながら、英語を話す人の助けをかりるにしたことはありませんが……）初めは、単語の意味をわかろうとする心配は、いりません。この書は音声のために選りすぐられたものであり、文脈を解する為のものではありません。

　　　　この本の個所は、以下のように分けられます；

　　　　ページ　1　においては、英語の基本となる音声があげられます。最初は基本音声の母音と子音から成り立ち、リストにあるすべての言葉は、ある他の表示事等を除いては、これらの音声が使われます。

　　　　ページ 17, 18, 19, 21, 22, 23　においては、この基本音声のリストのみが記されています。これらの音リストをマスターすれば、後の 67 ページから 118 ページの、アルファベットリストのもっと困難な音声を習得することができるでしょう。

英語を学ぶ方々へ：

　　この簡単な英語の音声のガイドは、さんがも困難に思われがちな発音と解読をマスターするのに役立つことと思われます。

　　全プログラムのかぎは、最初のページに記された音声の暗記と練習にあります。これらは英語を正確に話す上で必要な助けとなります。それから後は、独自で学習を続けられます。（しかしながら、英語を話す人の助けをかりるにしたことはありませんが……）初めは、単語の意味をわかろうとする心配は、いりません。この書は音声のために造りすぐられたものであり、文脈を解するためのものではありません。

　　この本の個所は、以下のように分けられます；

　　ページ 1 においては、英語の基本となる音声があげられます。最初は基本音声の母音と子音から成り立ち、リストにあるすべての言葉は、ある他の表示事等を除いては、これらの音声が使われます。

　　ページ＿＿＿＿＿＿＿＿においては、この本の音声のリストのみが記されています。これらの音リストをマスターすれば、後の 67 ページから 118。ページの、アルファベット リストのもっと困難な音声を習得することができるでしょう。

FOR PARENTS AND TEACHERS OF BEGINNING READERS

The teaching of reading to small children is a very delicate task. During the years in which sight-reading was in vogue, many children developed serious reading problems and some never learned to read at all. They just became more and more confused. Using a logical phonetic approach, children learn easily without confusion and without reading problems. Each child is an individual and his ability to learn to read may mature anywhere between their fourth and seventh year. This system itself will help you to know when they are ready.

To begin with, forget the A B C's, they have no relation with reality. Cat does not begin with C (see) but with ku. Why teach 'C'? Use the sounds given in the list on page 1 and teach only the small print letters, not capitals. (Since "a" has 5 sounds in English and 4 shapes; 2 prints and 2 scripts, it's no wonder the children get confused with an illogical reading program). If possible, buy or make tactile alphabets and let them feel each with the finger of their dominant hand as they learn them. Do not worry about teaching the alphabet in order; maybe start with the letters in their name. If their name is not phonetic as "GERALD", still teach the "g" of "gun". The other sounds will come later, after they are reading well. Teach only the 5 short vowel sounds and the basic consonants. That's all that is needed to be able to read. As they learn each letter sound, look for words that begin with that sound to start training their ears. (The Spanish consonants are almost the same as the English ones, so to read Spanish they only need to learn the vowel sounds, the double ll, rr and the ñ.)

If the child says that giraffe begins with ju it is right, don't correct them. When they recognize most of the alphabet, they can begin to write them. Remember that building the words with the letters comes long before reading so doesn't expect the child to read what they can form at first. If possible, use a cutout cardboard alphabet and have them form the three-letter phonetic words given in the first list. If you say "can" and the child does not hear the sounds Ku-aa-nn, then they are not ready for this step regardless of age. Certain paths in the brain need to mature before this step can be mastered and the best teacher in the world won't be able to help until this is done. Go back to having them tell you with what sounds different words begin with until you feel they can sound them out easily. You may help them learn to write by feeling the tactile letters and then forming them in the air, on your back or hand, using chalk or on a sand or salt tray before using pencil and paper.

Remember a four-year-old brain may be ready to read while a four-year-old hand may not be able to write and visa-versa.

When a child, using loose lower case letters, can form with ease the words from the first lists, then you can begin to work with the four-letter words from the second list. Instead of dictating them, find small picture cards or little objects and let them form the words beside them with the individual alphabet letters.

I find that practice forming about two hundred words is a good preparation for reading. The children themselves will show this ability when they are ready. Do not try to have them read before being able to form the words easily.

When ready for reading, the most important step in one's life, return to the three letter words and write one yourself on a small card, letting the child sound the letters out again and again until the word "pops" into their head. Practice all the 3 letters words before continuing with the blends and longer words. A long phonetic word will be easy for him, but don't try non-phonetic words yet. Work your way slowly through the first part of the book. At first, only read one word at a time and let them match the word to an object or picture.

Carefully printing each word and pasting them on white calling cards, will make it much easier for the child to read. Choose from each column about 10 words and work only with those until the child can write them with the moveable alphabet and later read them. Be sure to use as large a font as will fit on the card once they are reading. Before that you will only be using the picture cards or objects.

Finding the best picture to go with each word is so easy today, go to Google Images and you will find thousands to pick from. Cut them out and paste them on a blank calling card to match with the word card or to use with the alphabet.

Check your child's boxes of old toys and ask your friends for those of their children, visit thrift shops and garage sales to begin to collect small objects to use with the alphabet and later the words once they are reading.

Use fonts like Comic Sans that have this letter a as you do not want to confuse your beginning reader by using the printed a used in books not designed for early readers.

FIRST LEVEL
THREE LETTER PHONETIC WORDS

<u>a</u>

act	cad	jab	Nat	tat
adz	cam	jag	pad	tax
alb	can	jam	pal	van
alp	cap	Jan	Pam	vat
am	cat	lab	pan	wad
amp	dab	lad	pat	wag
an	Dad	lag	rag	wax
and	dam	lam	ram	yak
ant	fad	lap	ran	yam
apt	fag	lax	rap	yap
as	fat	Mac	rat	
ask	gab	mad	sad	
asp	gag	man	sag	
at	gap	map	Sam	
ax	gas	mat	sat	
bad	had	Max	tab	
bag	hag	nab	tad	
ban	ham	nag	tag	
bat	has	Nan	tan	
cab	hat	nap	tap	

A Practical Guide to Phonics

FIRST LEVEL cont...
THREE LETTER PHONETIC WORDS

e			**i**	
bed	leg	wed	bib	id
beg	let	wen	bid	if
Ben	Meg	wet	big	ilk
bet	men	yen	bin	imp
den	met	yes	bit	in
elf	net	yet	did	ink
elk	peg	yes	dim	is
elm	pen	yet	din	it
end	pep	Zeb	dip	jib
fed	pet	zed	fib	jig
fez	red		fig	Jim
get	Rex		fin	kid
hem	set		fit	Kim
hen	sex		fix	kin
hep	Ted		gig	kit
hex	ten		hid	lid
jet	Tex		him	lip
keg	vet		hip	lit
Ken	vex		his	Liz
led	web		hit	mid

FIRST LEVEL cont...
THREE LETTER PHONETIC WORDS

o

mix	vim	bob	hog	on
nib	wig	bog	hop	opt
nil	win	bop	job	ox
nip	wit	box	jog	pod
nit	yip	cob	Jon	pop
nix	zip	cod	jot	pot
pin		cog	lob	pox
pig		con	log	rob
pit		cop	lop	roc
rib		cot	lot	rod
Sid		doc	lox	Ron
sin		dog	mob	rot
sis		Don	Mom	sob
sit		dot	mot	tog
six		fog	mop	Tom
tic		fop	nob	top
Tim		fox	nod	tot
tin		god	nog	yom
tip		got	not	yon
tit		hot	om	

FIRST LEVEL cont...
THREE LETTER PHONETIC WORDS

u

bud	hum	run
bug	Hun	rut
bum	hut	tug
bun	jug	sub
bus	jut	sud
but	lug	sum
cub	lux	tun
cud	mud	sun
cup	mug	sup
cut	mum	tub
dub	nub	tux
dud	nun	up
dug	nut	us
dun	pub	yum
fun	pug	
gum	pun	
gun	pup	
Gus	pus	
Gut	rub	
hub	rug	
hug	rum	

SECOND LEVEL
LONGER PHONETIC WORDS AND
CONSONANT BLENDS

BLENDS: br, cl, cr, ct, dr, fl, fr, gl, gr, lb, lk, lt, mp, nk, nt, lp, pr, pt, sl, sk, st, str, sc, sp, spl, sw, tr, ts, wr.

<u>a</u>

act	clam	fast	haft	plan
apt	clamp	flag	hams	plank
bank	clan	flap	hand	plant
band	clank	flask	hank	pram
blab	clap	flat	Hans	rank
bland	clasp	flax	hasp	raft
blank	crab	flex	jack	ramp
blast	cram	Frank	lamp	rank
blat	crank	gasp	land	rasp
brad	damp	glad	lank	sand
brag	dank	grab	last	sank
bran	draft	graft	mask	scab
brand	drag	gram	mast	scalp
camp	dram	grand	pans	scat
cans	drank	grant	pant	scrap
cast	fact	grasp	past	slab
clad	fans	Greg	pend	slam

SECOND LEVEL cont...
LONGER PHONETIC WORDS AND CONSONANT BLENDS

BLENDS: br, cl, cr, ct, dr, fl, fr, gl, gr, lb, lk, lt, mp, nk, nt, lp, pr, pt, sl, sk, st, str, sc, sp, spl, sw, tr, ts, wr.

e

slap	swank	belt	fret	pent
smack	swat	bend	glen	pent
snag	tank	bent	heft	pest
snap	task	best	Helen	present
span	tamp	bled	held	rend
spank	tram	blend	helmet	rent
spat	tramp	clef	help	rest
splat	trap	crept	hemp	sect
stab	vamp	deft	kept	self
stag	vast	delft	left	send
stalk		dent	lend	sent
stamp		desk	lent	seven
stand		drempt	meld	sled
stat		egret	mend	slept
strap		emblem	neglect	smelt
strand		expect	nest	sped
swab		felt	next	spend
swam		fend	pelt	stem

SECOND LEVEL cont...
LONGER PHONETIC WORDS AND CONSONANT BLENDS

BLENDS: br, cl, cr, ct, dr, fl, fr, gl, gr, lb, lk, lt, mp, nk, nt, lp, pr, pt, sl, sk, st, str, sc, sp, spl, sw, tr, ts, wr.

i

step	welt	blimp	hint	insist
steps	wend	blink	drift	kilt
Stetson	went	blip	drink	kink
strep	wept	blitz	drip	lick
swept	west	bilk	film	lift
temp	yelp	bind	fist	limit
tempest		brim	frisk	limp
tend		brink	flint	link
tent		clinic	Fritz	lint
test		clink	gift	lips
text		clip	gild	list
veld		crib	gilt	livid
velvet		crimp	glib	midst
vend		crispin	glint	milk
vent		dint	grid	mink
vest		disk	grim	misft
weft		grip	grin	mishap
weld		hilt	insipid	misprint

A Practical Guide to Phonics

SECOND LEVEL cont...
LONGER PHONETIC WORDS AND CONSONANT BLENDS

BLENDS: br, cl, cr, ct, dr, fl, fr, gl, gr, lb, lk, lt, mp, nk, nt, lp, pr, pt, sl, sk, st, str, sc, sp, spl, sw, tr, ts, wr.

o

mist	silk	spritz	vivid	blob
picnic	silt	sprint	wind	bloc
pilgrims	sink	stilt	wink	blond
pink	skin	stink	wilt	blot
pint	skip	strict	wisp	bon-bon
pins	skit	strip	wist	bond
pistil	slid	swift		clod
prig	slim	swig		clogs
prim	slink	tilt		clop
primp	slip	timid		cost
print	slit	tint		crop
prism	snip	trim		drop
rift	spilt	trip		flog
rink	spin	twig		flop
risk	spit	twin		fond
scrimp	splint	twist		frog
scrip	split	victim		font
sift	sprig	visit		frond

SECOND LEVEL cont...
LONGER PHONETIC WORDS AND CONSONANT BLENDS

BLENDS: br, cl, cr, ct, dr, fl, fr, gl, gr, lb, lk, lt, mp, nk, nt, lp, pr, pt, sl, sk, st, str, sc, sp, spl, sw, tr, ts, wr.

u

frost	slop	blunt	fund	plus
golf	slot	bulb	glum	pulp
gong	smog	bump	glut	pump
grog	soft	bust	grub	rusk
loft	spot	club	grump	rust
lost	stomp	clump	gulf	scud
plod	stop	cupful	gulp	scrub
plot	trod	crust	gust	scum
plop	trot	duct	hump	skunk
pomp	tromp	dump	hunt	slug
pond		dunk	jump	slum
prod		dusk	just	smug
prompt		dust	lump	snub
prop		drug	mumps	snug
plot		drum	must	spud
romp		drunk	plug	stub
scot		flux	plum	stud
slog		frump	plunk	stump

A Practical Guide to Phonics

SECOND LEVEL cont...
LONGER PHONETIC WORDS AND CONSONANT BLENDS

BLENDS: br, cl, cr, ct, dr, fl, fr, gl, gr, lb, lk, lt, mp, nk, nt, lp, pr, pt, sl, sk, st, str, sc, sp, spl, sw, tr, ts, wr.

stun
stunk
strum
strut
suds
swum
trust
tuft
tusk
trump
trunk
uncut
unjust
unplug

First Reading Lesson

READING TWO AND THREE WORD PHRASES

When the child is reading single words easily, introduce word phrases. To make it more fun, start with single verbs from the lists and write them on individual cards and have them act out the commands as they read them. Two or more children can act them out to each other. Samples are given below. After the verb phrases, give them adjective and prepositions phrases to enforce the reading of every word in a phrase, not only the larger. Here it is necessary to teach "a", "I" and "the" as sight words. The child will begin to use flash cards.

Examples: First group uses single verbs found in the first two pages of lists; three letter words and blends. Second group uses two word phrases. If the child writes them, have them read the words, act them out, then turn over the card and write them from memory. Here you may teach them to leave spaces between words by putting their finger between each word.

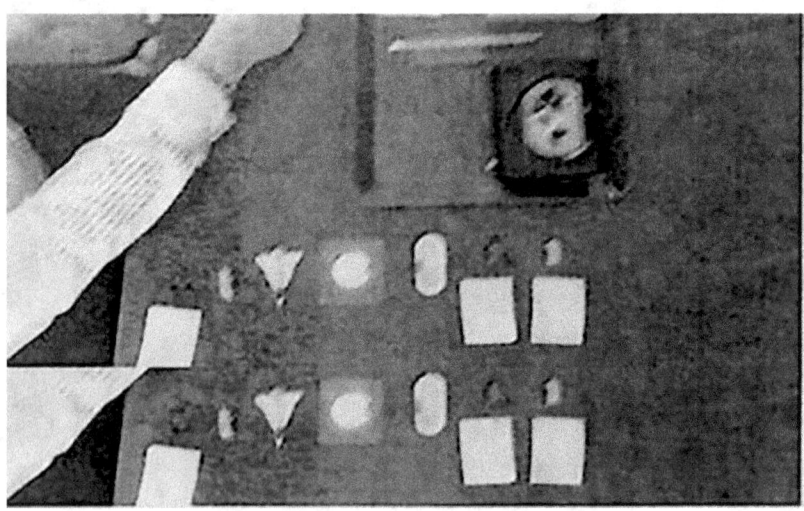

SECOND GROUP
USES TWO WORD PHRASES

act glad	jump up	unplug lamp
act mad	lick lips	
act sad	lift flag	
act sick	melt jam	
ax elm	nag Dan	
back up	pat dog	
bat bug	run fast	
can plums	scat cat	
clap hands	scrub sink	
cut bud	sit up	
dent can	skim milk	
dip cup	snip frond	
drag mop	spank Sam	
drink milk	stand up	
fan Dad	step up	
fix bed	stop pranks	
gag Ted	swim fast	
get mat	tag Jim	
get Mom	tilt cup	
help Dad	trim twig	
hunt fox	tug van	
hug Mom	unpin clasp	

THIRD GROUP USES "AND"
(THREE WORD PHRASES)

act and hum
blend and mix
blink and wink
grab on and yank
hit and jab
hop and skip
jab and hit
jump and clap
jump and run
jump and sit
lend and spend
lent and spent
mix and sup
nod yes and no
plod and rest
plod and trip
press and trim
rub and tap
run and stop
run and win
sit and grin
sift and mix
skip and jump
stand and sit
twist and hop
wag and yap

FOURTH GROUP
INTRODUCTION OF "A" AS A WORD IN ITSELF

ask a nun
beg a bun
bet a lot
blot a spot
blunt a tip
cram a box
dust a cabin
cut a ham
cut a mask
draft a text
drink a cupful
drink a drop
drip a drop
film a pilgrim
fix a flat
flap a flag
fund an act
gas a van
get a bon bon
get a pink pig

grasp a hand
lift a lid
melt a mint
mist a plant
net a bug
pat a cat
pin a print
plug a tap
press a scrap
rest on a blanket
rub a dub dub
run a zig-zag
run up a ramp
sand a desk
scrub a sink
sit on a mat
spin a top
stop a cab
stop a plot

top a pup
stop an unjust man
sip a cupful
tan a hand
tilt a blimp
top a jar
trap a fox
trip an imp
trust a man
twist a wisp
vex an adult
wax a raft
wet a spot
wig a scalp

FIFTH GROUP
ADJECTIVE PHRASES
IF POSSIBLE FIND PICTURES AND OBJECTS TO MATCH
INTRODUCTION OF "THE" AS A SIGHT WORD.

a deft mom	the damp mink
a cut scrap	the dim bulb
a fast hand	the dust pan
a fast trot	the dust rag
a gilt helmet	the fat cat
a glad man	the fat man
a grand club	the flat man
a grand win	the fond twin
a kind man	the last drop
a log cabin	the left hand
a lost sled	the pink pig
a red felt	the pink crab
a red dog	the red fox
a red plum	the red stamp
a red rod	the scot clan
a sad man	the seven
a soft velvet	milkmen
a tan cat	the swift stab
a vivid tint	the tan desk
an uncut bud	the tin man
the avid band	the trim raft
the bank fund	the trim swan
the bent twig	the vast land
the blank print	

SIXTH GROUP
PREPOSITION PHRASES
IF POSSIBLE FIND PICTURES TO MATCH WITH THE PHRASES

bud on plant
cat in can
milk in pad
pig in pen
bud in pod
dust on rag
hams in pans
swim in tank
jump on ramp
twig on plant
dump in can
plug in plug
sink in pond
ham on bun
strut in step
cubs in dens
hop on pop
hats on men
trust in self
caps on kids
slot in bank
pigs in pens
swim in pond
men on rafts
brag in club
rats in traps
lost in cabin
frost on steps
stand on steps
top hat in box

sand in sandbox
mask on dentist
hand in hand
skunk in trap
crank on pump
tap on drum
hot dog on bun
milk in jug
Tom on top
ox in mud
bun in hut
fan on rug
bug on web
yen in hand
mud in bog
stag in fog
map on mat
run on mat
stand on bump
man on ramp
the cat on the mat
print on stubs
a hand in a fist
a cat in a can
a milkman in a van
a cat on a mat
insist on the best
the ham in the can
the cat in the sun
a hat on a man

the rim on a cup
the skunk in a box
a man on a raft
the jest in the sun
an elf on an elm
jump on a raft
the grip on an ax
a spot on a print
fun in the sun
an ax in a log
a rip in a vest
a ring on a hand
a cut on a leg
a tint on a lip
a visit in a camp
a bump on a log
snap on a mask
the wind in the elms
a grub on a frond
seven in a crib
a man midst men

SENTENCES

When the child is reading the phrases well, she/he may now be given the capital letters. Make a set of capital letters and on equal-size cards, a set of small letters. Show them how to put the small letters on a mat in alphabetical order, keeping the cards with the capitals in your hand. When they have finished putting them in two or three columns, show them the capital letters one at a time and have them match them to the small letter. He/she can write them if they wish.

Up until now most of the reading has been technical, the child is reading mechanically. Understanding the phrases they have read is another skill altogether. This is why it is important to match the phrases to pictures as they go along.

If at any point they seem to have problems, do more exercises. As the old saying goes, "go slowly, I'm in a hurry". Several short lessons may be more effective than long ones. Some children gallop along and some very bright ones trip up in the most unexpected places. I have never had a child **NOT** learn to read using this method but there may be a three- year span in any group of children from 4 to 7 between the first reader and the last.

Now comes the really big jump to sentences and books. Ideally small books could be made for every step of the way from the first three-letter one-word, one-page lists. It is impossible to call a book an early-reader when the first pages have words like "see", "look", "Jane", etc.; none of which are phonetic. None of the books on the supermarket shelves are phonetic. Even books that call themselves phonetic are not, because the words used have mixed phonograms.

When the child is reading the phrases well, she/he may now be given the capital letters. Make a set of capital letters and on equal-size cards, a set of small letters. Show them how to put the small letters on a mat in alphabetical order, keeping the cards with the capitals in your hand. When they have finished putting them in two or three columns, show them the capital letters one at a time and have them match them to the small letter. He/she can write them if they wish.

Up until now most of the reading has been technical, the child is reading mechanically. Understanding the phrases they have read is another skill altogether. This is why it is important to match the phrases to pictures as they go along.

If at any point they seem to have problems, do more exercises. As the old saying goes, "go slowly, I'm in a hurry". Several short lessons may be more effective than long ones. Some children gallop along and some very bright ones trip up in the most unexpected places. I have never had a child NOT learn to read using this method but there may be a three- year span in any group of children from 4 to 7 between the first reader and the last.

Now comes the really big jump to sentences and books. Ideally small books could be made for every step of the way from the first three-letter one-word, one-page lists. It is impossible to call a book an early-reader when the first pages have words like "see", "look", "Jane", etc.; none of which are phonetic. None of the books on the supermarket shelves are phonetic. Even books that call themselves phonetic are not, because the words used have mixed phonograms.

am an I a man tan No Yes ?
am an I a cat fat No Yes ?
am I a pig big ?.

This lesson should be given individually.

Tell the child, "First you learned letters, then words, and then we made phrases out of the words. Now you are going to tell something with the words, you are going to make sentences."

Take the small cards from the lists in this order and place them in front of him/her. Have them read them as you do so.

I am a dog.
I am an elf.

"I am a dog"... The words are telling you something and then they stop. We must put this little dot to say that they are finished. (Put the period sign) This is called a period. (Full stop.) Do another... "I am an elf" "I am a big dog". Each one tells something. Have him read them. Each time give him a period and remind him what it is and where to put it.

Then make a new sentence. "Am I a fat pig" and give him the question mark. "In this sentence they are not telling you, they are asking you, so you must put a "question mark" at the end and you must answer: "No, I am a man". Tell them that all sentences begin with capital letters.

Am I a fat pig?
No I am a man.

Now come the problems. The child is ready for reading but there are no books for him to read unless you write them as he may be a year away from reading so-called early- readers. I recommend the "Sullivan Programmed Reading" put out by Phoenix Learning Resources.

SIMPLE RULES

1. **SHORT VOWEL** The short vowels are those taught on page xiii, "Sounds of the English Language" in the first column. They are the sounds considered "phonetic" and have no symbol above them. If a word has only one vowel and it comes at the beginning or in between consonants, the vowel is usually short. (All of the words listed up to here use short vowels.) The dictionary symbol for a short vowel is a breve, ă, ĕ, ĭ, ŏ, ŭ.

3. **"Y" AS A CONSONANT** When Y comes at the beginning of a word, it is a consonant. (Yes, Yet)

4. **CONSONANT BLENDS** Two or three consonant sounds that blend together; BR, CL, CR, CT, DR, FL, FR, GL, GR, LB, LK, LT, MP, NK, NT, LP, PR, PT, SL, SK, ST, STR, SC, SP, SW, TR, TS, WR.

5. **DOUBLE CONSONANTS** Teaching double consonants is easy as the two sounds become one. BB, CK, DD, FF, GG, LL, MM, NN, PP, SS, TT, ZZ. For "K" and "CK" the rule is: After a vowel use "CK", and after a consonant use "K" (chick, brink).

6. **CONSONANT DIAGRAPHS** Two consonants together that make one sound that is different from the original separate sounds: SH, WH, TH, NG, TH, CH, KN, QU, PH.

7. **MURMUR DIPTHONGS** Vowels followed by "R": AR, ER, IR, OR, and UR. ER, IR and UR sound phonetic "r", "aR" sounds both their names; long ā + long "R". "oR" sounds both letters blended; long ō + **long R**.

8. **LONG VOWELS** The long vowels are those taught on page xiii in the second column. They are the old-fashioned "ABC's" and A, E, I, O and U are taught as we were taught. When teaching those to small children we say that phonetic "a" is the sound of the letter and long "ā" is the name of the letter. In many cases the vowel says its name instead of the sound. If a syllable has two vowels together, the first vowel is usually long and the second vowel is silent. When working with the child, we say that the second vowel makes the first say its name and then is silent. (Fēed, Bēan) this is also true with ending "E". (āpe, ēve, rīde, bōne, cūbe). If a syllable has only one vowel, and it comes at the end of a word, that vowel is usually long. (nō, alsō, gō). The dictionary symbol for a long vowel is called a micron. ā, ē, ī, ō, ū.

9. **"Y" AS A VOWEL** When "Y" comes at the end of two syllable words, it sounds long "ē" (bunny). When it comes at the end of a one-syllable word it sounds long "ī". (by, cry). Throughout this book a majority of the words in the columns use the long "ē" rule of words. On the occasions when the "y" sounds long ī at the end of a one-syllable word, it will be indicated next to the word: (y = long ī) or (y=ī).

10. **PLAIN DIPTHONGS** The different sound made when certain vowels blend together into one: (OI, EU, OU).

11. **REGULAR VOWEL DIAGRAPHS** The long vowel rule (āi, ēe, ēa, īe, ōa, āe).

12. **IRREGULAR VOWEL DIAGRAPHS** Two vowels together that have their own sound. (ŏŏ, ōō,—bŏŏk, pōōl).

13. **DOUBLE CONSONANTS WITH ING** If the verb is only one syllable long with a simple short vowel and the word ends in a consonant, you double the final consonant before adding ing (stop-stopping; hop-hopping).

14. When the children have finished working up to here, they are ready for the phonograms in the second part of the book, (pages 1 through 357). Now all the names of the letters (long ā, ē, ī, ō, ū) and all the sounds on page xiii need to be taught as the children will be using them to decode the phonograms.

15. Each phonogram has two parts, the first, a list of words only using that phonogram (with teacher made picture cards) and the second, a group of sentences also using that specific phonogram. The other words in each sentence are phonetic. It is important to teach a few of the most used phonograms first in order to use them when teaching the others.

Pages 1-13 start with the double consonants and all of these should be taught as the first steps. They are easy as the two consonants sound as one.

Then the ā-e, ē-e, ī-e, ō-e, ū-e; th, ar, er, ir, or and ur: and the words from the be, do, th, sh, ā, ē, ī, ō, and ū lists. Was, were, when, where, how; why, the three "ed" sounds; "ow"; the three "y" sounds, all are used often. You can add any others to your lists, there is no rule. Use them as you need them or how they are found in a reading book.

To teach these new sound combinations, use two different colored moveable alphabets. The phonogram to be taught is from one box, and the rest of the word from the other. Using small objects or cards with pictures, have the child write the word in two colors and, using two different colored pencils, copy them in a notebook.

The next step is to write them inside folded calling cards with the rule on the outside. The child takes one, looks inside and reads it, then puts the "tent" down and tries to write it. They should check it by themselves. The last step is for them to read the sentences aloud to you. This will tell you if they have learned the correct pronunciation.

SOUNDS AND SENTENCES

Double Consonants

bb
dobbin
ebb
hubbub
rabbit

tt
Emmett

gg
biggest
egg
ugg
yegg

mm
gimmick
summer
summit

nn
Ann
banns
bonnet
Ennis
inn
kennels
tannin
tennis

zz
buzz
fizz
fuzz
razz

Sentences Double Consonants

bb = b, mm = m, nn = n, tt = t

Fix the webbing for the nibbling rabbit and stop bobbing Dobbin.

Emmett's summer gimmick is swimming at the brimming pond and bumming and cramming his lunch.

In the summit hut, Emma is humming and hemming her bonnet and trimming the dimming lamp.

Connan and Ennis, banning the winning tennis inning went running to the kennels.

Grinning, Ann, in a sunning bonnet went without tanning to the inn.

Sentences Double Consonants

gg = g, zz = z

His leggings slipped from lugging and tugging the logging rigging onto the sagging bogging land.

The slugging and mugging is bugging the digging men in the fogging dusk.

Hugging, and hopping; jigging and jogging; and then begging, his lagging lad kept him from tagging his leg.

Nagging and haggling but not hogging or pigging out, his bagging was finished.

Buzzing, fizzing and razzing, was Fuzzy's grand razz-ma-tazz!

Double Consonants
ck= k

back	jacket	sack
black	jock	sick
blick	kick	slick
block	lack	smack
brick	lick	smock
buck	lock	snack
bucket	luck	sock
clock	muck	stack
cluck	nack	stock
crack	neck	struck
cricket	Nick	stuck
deck	pack	tack
duck	packet	tick
duckling	peck	ticket
fleck	pick	tock
flick	picket	track
flock	pluck	trick
fleck	quack	truck
frock	rack	tack
hock	rock	Vick
Jack	Rick	wick

Sentences Double Consonants

ck = k

Ducks quack, hens cluck, chicks peck, clocks tick-tock, bricks crack and kids lick.

Stack the stock of frocks on the rack next to the packed sack of black rocks.

The jock struck the mud and his truck stuck smack in the slick track of muck.

A flock of crickets can kick their back legs and flick off the dock.

Rub Vicks on sick Nick's back and neck, get his wet socks off, and bring him a snack.

His nack of flicking off a lit wick with a few flecks can bring him luck.

Pluck a packet of trick tickets tacked on to Rick's jacket in his locker.

Jack's best luck is the black cricket in his pocket.

Double Consonants

dd
add
addict
address
odd
redden
sudden

pp
happen
happiness

ff
biff
bluff
cliff
coffin
cuff
fluff
gruff
huff
Jeff
luff
Muff
muffin
off
offend

puff
riff-raff
ruff
scoff
scruff
scuff
sniff
snuff
staff
stiff
stuff
suffix
traffic

Sentences Double Consonants

ff = f, pp = p, dd = d

Sco**ff**ing, the ri**ff**-ra**ff** o**ff**ended Bi**ff** the tra**ff**ic cop, and blu**ff**ed himself into his car.

His is the co**ff**in after his jump o**ff** the cli**ff** blu**ff**.

Sni**ff**ing, Mu**ff** led Je**ff** by the scru**ff** of his neck to the mu**ff**in man.

Hu**ff**ing and pu**ff**ing, the fl**uff**y, gr**uff** dog r**uff**ed and sni**ff**ed the man's c**uff**ed hand and sta**ff**.

Ha**pp**iness ha**pp**ens.

Su**dd**enly it a**dd**s up; get the a**dd**ress of the o**dd** a**dd**ict with the re**dd**ened hands and run him to the deck.

Double Consonants

ll

bell	kill	till
Bill	lull	well
cell	mill	will
cull	mull	yell
dell	nill	
doll	pell	
dull	pill	
drill	pull	
dwell	quill	
Ellis	rill	
Ellen	scull	
fell	sell	
fill	sill	
full	skill	
gill	skull	
grill	smell	
gull	spell	
hill	spill	
hull	still	
ill	swell	
Jill	tell	

Sentences Double Consonants

ll = l

Bill is yelling as the doll fell pell-mell from the hill and spilled into the dell.

Run Ellen, a pill, as Jill is ill and pull a rill on the bell to call the drill.

Scull his hull on the still swell 'till I can tell that the lull will stop.

Ellis will dwell in the dull cell 'till Bill can grill him on killing the skull in the well.

Cull the hulls with skill and fill the mill full but do not spill a bit of the full mull.

Tell Jill to null the smell of the quills; do not sell smelly quills.

On the spelling drill Will did spell skill, gill and gull.

Double Consonants

ss		**tt**
ass	mass	attempt
Bess	mess	attic
bless	miss	batten
boss	moss	butt
brass	Ness	jutt
class	pass	kitten
cress	puss	mitten
cross	press	mutt
dismiss	Ross	putt
dress	stress	rotten
glass	Swiss	watt
gloss	toss	
guess		
grass		
fossil		
fuss		
hiss		
kiss		
lass		
less		
loss		

Sentences Double Consonants

ss = s, tt = t

Missing mass, Bess lost her cross and was not blessed as when crossing the pass Ross tossed her into the mossy grass.

The brassy boss dismissed the class guessing that the glass mess was stressful.

The assistant Swiss miss pressed her hissing pussycat to her dress and fussed and kissed him.

His loss of the glossy Lock Ness fossil was less than the loss of his lass.

Put on mittens and attempt to batten the jutting buttresses.

The mutt and the kitten were in the attic putting

Dictionary of Sounds and Sentences

The next page begins the lists in alphabetical order of the combinations of sounds (phonograms).

In the lists and sentences, only the phonogram to be taught is used. In this way the sounds are reinforced without any other combinations of sounds to confuse the student.

I only used phonetic, easily pronounced words in the code page, something dictionaries do not do.

Definition of phonogram, Wikipedia: (linguistics) *A group of letters which share the same letter combination associated with a sound.*

a_e = long ā_silent e

ale	gate	plane	vase
ape	grade	plate	wade
ate	grape	rake	wake
babe	grate	rave	wave
bake	grave	raven	
blade	graze	safe	
blame	hate	sale	
blaze	insane	same	
brave	jade	save	
cake	Jake	scale	
came	Jane	scrape	
cane	lake	shade	
cape	lame	shape	
case	lane	skate	
cave	late	slave	
crane	lemonade	slate	
crave	make	spade	
dame	male	stale	
date	mate	take	
drake	maze	tale	
fate	name	tame	
flake	pale	tape	
flame	pavement	trade	

Sentences
a_e = long ā_silent e

Jake and Jane came up safe after a skate scrape on the pavement.

The brave ape and his date mate ate baked cake on a plate.

His dame has a lame tame crane; his dame has a crane that is lame.

Babe, take a spade and a rake and wade in the lake and make the gate to the grate safe.

Blame the same insane pale male for the blaze of flame.

I hate the shade of that plate; take it in trade for a vase.

The tale is that the raven came in the cave maze as his grave fate.

a #1 = ä

ability	banana	mama
Adela	coca cola	rather
adorn	disappoint	relative
Africa	Donna	sepia
Alma	Elsa	Stella
along	Eva	squash
Amada	extra	swamp
amazement	fauna	swan
amend	father	swat
America	flora	umbrella
antenna	grandfather	vodka
Aladdin	Greta	want
arithmetic	ha	water
assist	Isabel	zebra
astonishment	Israel	vanilla
attack		

Sentences
a #1 = ä

Adela's ability to assist Alma to adorn the sepia map of America left Elsa gasping in amazement.

Eva, do not disappoint grandfather Aladdin in that arithmetic test.

The flora and fauna (zēbras) of Africa astonishes Stella's relative from Israel.

Father, get an umbrella and go into the swamp to swat and squash bugs.

Ha, ha, Isabel, go along, as Amada can amend her attack on Greta's antenna.

Donna wants a vanilla and banana Coca-Cola without vodka.

The swans rather want extra water.

Mama Cass sings pop songs.

a #2 = long ä

April
avis
behavior
cradle
crazy
David
favor
flavor
haste
ladle
lady
ladybug
lazy
making
Octavius
paper
savior
shady

a #3 = e

Evans
marshmallow
shall
servant

Sentences a #3 = e

Shall Evan's servant get marshmallows?

a #4 = i (y = ē)

any

many

Sentences a #4 = i (y = ē)

Any is not many.

a #5 = u
(-able words have silent e)

academic	Ballad	Sabbath
across	Connan	salad
adrift	Duncan	Vulcan
another	lullaby (y=long ī)	what
atlas	oracle	was
attack	relative	

Sentences a #5 = u

Another oracle sent Connan to attack Atlas and Vulcan in a battle.

What was this Sabbath oracle, another attack on his ballad?

What was fantastic was that Duncan attacked the odd verdant salad plants.

Sad Atlas was set adrift across the gulf. The ballad of Connan the Barbarian was odd. Sing that small relative a lullaby.

The academic was a significant narrator on the Sabbath

able = uble (silent e)

attach**able**
bank**able**
bill**able**
drink**able**
despic**able**
elect**able**
forgiv**able**
hitt**able**
humm**able**
kiss**able**
match**able**
miser**able**
pass**able**
pack**able**
patch**able**
remark**able**
respect**able**
unthink**able**

Sentences
able = uble (silent e)

That humm**able** song will be bank**able**.

His fastball is hit**table** but his best ball is just pass**able**.

This skirt is match**able** with that shirt and is attach**able** to that pack**able** jacket.

It is forgiv**able** to get drink**able** drinks from undrink**able** ponds if simmered.

His pants are patch**able** if they get match**able** swatches first.

I had some match**able** swatches.

able = long ā + bul (silent e)

able
fable
Mable
markable
marketable
sable
stable
table
unable

Sentences
able = long ā + bul (silent e)

In the fable, **able** **Mable** had **sables** in her **stables**.

Mable was un**able** to scrub the **stables** with the **sables** in the stalls.

The **sables** were market**able** so **Mable** was **able** to market them.

Then **Mable** did scrub the **stables** and got extra market**able** **sables**.

As the **sables** were mark**able** **Mable** remark**ably** marked them with red ink.

The red ink marked the **sables** and then they were not market**able**.

Mable then did not get a **sable** jacket so she kept all the **sables** in the **stable**.

ace = long ā + s (silent e)

ace
brace
bracelet
disgrace
displace
embrace
face
grace
interface
lace
mace
misplace
pace
place
race
replace
space
trace
unlace

Sentences
ace = long ā + s (silent e)

Ace fa**ce**d that he had mispla**ce**d Ann's la**ce** with no tra**ce** and bra**ce**d himself to fa**ce** disgra**ce**.

Then **Ace** ra**ce**d to repla**ce** Ann's la**ce** and pla**ce** a bra**ce**let in its spa**ce**.

Ann with gra**ce** did not disgra**ce** **Ace** but hugged and embra**ce**d him.

Repla**ce** the interfa**ce** in its spa**ce**.

Unla**ce** his tennis racket and repla**ce** the strings.

Ann had a tra**ce** of ma**ce** on her la**ce** so pla**ce**d it in water to displa**ce** the smell.

I **ace**d it!

age #1 = long ā + j (silent e)

age
ages
cage
engage
enrage
gage
page
rage
sage
wage

Sentences
age #1 = long ā + j (silent e)

"Rock of **ages**", is a song that eng**ages** the **sage's** spirit.

Enr**age**d, the **age**d man spotted his dog in a c**age**.

Do not get in a r**age** as the c**age** is not shut and has a bed.

The **sage's page** asked for a small w**age**. At that **age** a **sage** gets a bad w**age**.

Nan was eng**age**d for **ages**.

That **page** has the g**ages** for the **sage's** experiment.

The **ages** pass and men still eng**age** in r**ages** and the land sobs.

age #2 = ej (silent e)

advant**age**
bagg**age**
band**age**
bever**age**
cabb**age**
cott**age**
dam**age**
im**age**
man**age**
marri**age**
mess**age**
pass**age**
sav**age**
stor**age**
vant**age**
vill**age**

Sentences
age #2 = ej (silent e)

I lived in a village cottage after marriage and had a cabbage patch.

In passage to the village, a savage dog bit mē and I had to get a bandage.

The advantage was that I managed to hit him with this baggage.

I did the dog no damage but now my image will send him from the village.

Yes, I had a hot beverage and sent a message to the village of the damage.

I was bringing the baggage to the advantage storage in the village.

Then I went back to my village cottage.

ah=ä

b**ah**
Debor**ah**
fell**ah**
Hann**ah**
Hezeki**ah**
hurr**ah**
huzz**ah**
Kasb**ah**
matz**ah**
Savann**ah**
Verand**ah**

Sentences ah=ä

Bah! Hannah has better Matzah balls than Deborah.

Hurrah! Huzzah! Hezekiah is back from the Kasbah.

The rajah stands on his verandah to call his fellah from the Savannah.

Hezekiah has a fellah to bring him the Torah on the Sabbath.

Deborah wants to go back to Savannah.

"Hard-Hearted Hannah, the Vamp from Savannah" was Bev's kin.

Yell six huzzahs for Savannah, Hurrah, Hurrah, Hurrah"

ai = long ā

aid	Gail	plain
ail	gain	rail
aim	grain	raisin
bait	hail	sails
braid	jail	saint
brain	laid	snail
Craig	maiden	staid
chain	mail	stain
claim	main	strain
daisy	nail	tail
exclaim	paid	train
explain	pail	vain
fail	pain	wait
faint	paint	waist

Sentences
ai = long ā

"Wait", exclaimed vain Gail, "I got the sails in the mail from Craig's List but they were stained."

"I paid for ten and aimed to paint them", explained the plain maiden faintly, "but a pail of strained paint failed to aid us."

Braid a daisy chain into a pigtail and train it to fall to the staid saint's waist.

His main ail was he claimed that his brain had pains from being laid in jail.

Hail, the last nail in the rail was gained at snail's swiftness.

ain = en

again
bargain
chaplain
captain
certainly
certain
curtain
fountain
mountain
plantain

Sentences ain = en

Again the captain is bargaining with the villain.

The chaplain certainly wants to plant plantains on the mountain.

The villain wants to curtain the plants with bricks and blocks.

I am certain that fountains will be better for the mountain.

The plantains will get bigger and taller and help wet the mountain.

Mountains are certainly best when verdant.

The captain and the chaplain will win the bargain with the villain.

air = âr

air
airy
chair
dairy
despair
fair
fairly
fairy
flair
hair
impair
lair
repair
stair
pair
unfair

Sentences
air = âr

The fairy despaired to get to her chair and repair her fair hair.

In the air the fairy was impaired from fixing her hair.

It was unfair that the airy lair of that fair fairy was fairly impaired.

A pair of dairymen repaired the stair to the fairy chair.

The fairy king with flair went to visit the attractive fairy.

Of all Fairylands the fair hair of yon fairy is the fairest.

That fairy is the fairest of the fair.

al #1 = aw

chalk
stalk
talk
walk

Sentences al #1 = aw

Sam hid the chalk and went for a walk.

Stalk but do not talk, just walk.

al #2 = awl

all
bald
ball
Baltic
call
calm
fall
falter
false (silent e)
hall
halter
mall
malt
Malta
Oswald
pall
Ronald
salt
scald
small
stall
tall
wall
walnut
Walter
waltz

Sentences
al #2 = awl

Small Walter, bald Oswald, and calm Ronald did falter at the mall's costs for the walnuts.

Hang the halter on the wall in Champ's stall and then wash it all with scalding salt.

Ronald mixed his pet a small mug of walnut malt.

The false wall in the hall made Walter falter and call for help.

At the Baltic ball, all the Malta men did waltz with calm polish.

To not fall, Walter must not falter at all.

Ronald did not win after all as a false call of the ball's fall left him faltering.

Oswald the rabbit and Ronald McDonald called for malted milk in the Mall's hall kitchen.

All went to the Mall in an attempt to get small balls for the Fall Pall Mall waltz.

al #3 = ul

alas
along
animal
capital
criminal
Donald
Emerald
finally
general
hospital
immortal
lateral
metal
pedal
petal
Randal
rascal
sandal
several
signal

Sentences
al #3 = ul

Alas, along went Donald with that rascal Randal and so did his capital.

Donald did not spot his sister, Emerald.

Emerald's signal was that Randal was a criminal.

That rascal robbed several silver metals Randal had as well as his sandals.

Emerald thinks that Randal is as bad as an animal and that he will finally end up in the General Hospital.

Randal thinks that rascals are immortal.

His instrument's lateral pedal is missing.

ang = long ā + nj

change
danger
mange
manger
ranger
stranger

Sentences
ang = long ā + nj

The ranger indicated the danger in a dog having mange.

That stranger changed his manger to stop the dangerous mange.

Phonograms

ant = unt

constant
elegant
expectantly
hesitant
important
indignant
infant
infantry
inhabitant
pennant
redundant
reluctant
stagnant
tenant

Sentences
ant = unt

The infantryman constantly held the elegant pennant.

It is important to not be hesitant as the children expectantly think the pennant will pass them.

The infantrymen marched with the pennants and the reluctant tenant indignantly thinks it redundant to have ten pennants.

The inhabitants held their infants up as the pennants passed.

The infantrymen think it is important to march elegantly bordering the inhabitants and not as if stagnant.

ar #1 = R

arctic	darn	part
arf	dart	scar
ark	far	scarf
arm	farm	shark
army	garden	sharp
art	garment	smart
artist	hard	snarl
artistic	hark	spar
bar	harm	spark
barb	harmful	star
bark	harp	stark
barn	harvest	swarm
car	jar	tar
card	lark	target
Cardiff	mar	tart
carpet	mark	war
cart	mars	warm
Clark	mart	warn
dark	parent	yard
darling	park	yarn

Sentences
ar #1 = R

Start the car darling, and park it in the garden yard.

Arf, arf, barks and snarls the dog to warn of harm in the stark dark.

A lark sang in the barnyard to mark the farm harvest.

Hard at war far in the Arctic the army targets that part of Cardiff.

Smart Barbs, Clark's star artist, darns with yarn the sparkling garment.

His tar mark will mar part of the warm artistic scarf.

Darling, hark the harp in the starlit garden park.

ar #2 = er

awkward	lizard
backward	Mary
blizzard	mustard
buzzard	orchard
caterpillar	ordinary
collar	Oscar
coward	pillar
custard	sugar
dullard	standard
Edward	toward
forward	upward
Haggar	vulgar
Hubbard	wizard
inward	westward
laggard	

Sentences
ar #2 = er

It was awkward when Oscar tripped backward into Haggard.

The standard for that job is not for dullards or laggards.

Mary was lost in the orchard when the blizzard struck and Edward went westward toward her wayward path.

The lizard had the caterpillar for lunch and then the buzzard had the lizard for his lunch.

Custard the dragon was a coward but the wizard was as valiant as mustard.

Twist your collar inward to not be forward, ordinary or vulgar.

A pillar of ordinary sugar is sugary.

ar #3 = âr

Barry
carry
contrary
daring
Harry
Karen
Larry
marry
ordinary
parry
secretary
tarry
vary
wary

Sentences
ar #3 = âr

Barry, carry Karen, and do not tarry, as Karen is no ordinary singer.

On the contrary, Harry, nary an ordinary individual is daring to kick that ball.

That secretary tarries too much, be wary.

Tarry, Harry for daring to marry that ordinary secretary.

The facts will vary but that fast secretary will send the ordinary letters.

Larry, parry his daring thrust as that wary man is much better.

Karen will not tarry but will do a daring parry to win.

That harry dog is no ordinary mutt as it can carry wary Larry on its back.

Barry has to pick up Harry and Larry and carry them to that daring man's festival.

are = âr

bare	hardware
blare	mare
care	prepare
careless	rare
compare	scare
dare	share
fare	snare
farewell	spare
flare	stare
glare	tare
grandparent	ware
hare	welfare

Sentences
are = âr

Nick will prepare the mare for a rare farewell.

Ned's scare will put him on bare welfare. His grandparent glared at the careless job.

Do not spare his ware but care for the bare fare.

Compare the careless hardware to prepare the mare's fare.

Share his spare ware with Sam, but do not let him be careless.

His grandparent stared at the flare that they prepared to scare all the careless hares.

His grandparent glared at the careless job.

ation = long ā + shun

admir**ation**
constell**ation**
dict**ation**
dil**ation**
don**ation**
el**ation**
escal**ation**
fix**ation**
hesit**ation**
inform**ation**
imagin**ation**
invit**ation**
lig**ation**

litig**ation**
n**ation**
not**ation**
ov**ation**
organiz**ation**
quot**ation**
rel**ation**
starv**ation**
st**ation**
tax**ation**
zonific**ation**
vac**ation**

Sentences
ation = long ā + shun

When he went on vac**ation**, he got the inform**ation** of the escal**ation** of his zonific**ation** and tax**ation** so he went to litig**ation**.

Ned's admir**ation** of the rel**ations** of the constell**ations** brings his el**ation** and fix**ation**.

That **nation**'s first-rate organiz**ation** and imagin**ation** sent don**ations** to stop starv**ation**.

As in Sam's not**ation**, he did a dict**ation** to send an invit**ation** for the escal**ation** of their ov**ation** with a quot**ation** of their **nation**'s successful s**tation**.

I have no hesit**ation** to ask for the ov**ation** as the ra**tions** of those at starv**ation** levels in that na**tion** have had a big dil**ation**.

au = å

applaud
augur
August
aunt
Austin
cauldron
daub
fault
fraud
gaunt
haul
haunted
jaunt
mauve
nautical
Paul
taunt
staunch
vault

Sentences
au = å

Applaud gaunt, staunch **Aunt Paula**; do not taunt her as a fraud.

He has to haul a lot to **Austin** this **August** to staunch the kid's mauve daubs.

The nautical fault was in not fixing the faulty vault for **Paul's** jaunt.

The augurs are bad for frauds in the **August** jaunt.

Paul's fraud taunted all with a haunted cauldron.

augh #1 = ä

aught
caught
daughter
draught
draughty
fraught
haughtily
haughty
naughty
taught

Sentences
augh #1 = ä

Dan **augh**t to have c**augh**t and t**augh**t his h**augh**ty, n**augh**ty d**augh**ter.

No man with **augh**t on his mind and fr**augh**t with terror can be t**augh**t.

Checkers can be called dr**augh**ts.

The dr**augh**ty mist c**augh**t up the man fr**augh**t with terror.

augh #2 = af

l**augh**   l**augh**ed   l**augh**ter

Sentences
augh #2 = af

Jim l**augh**ed and l**augh**ed and his l**augh**ter made all the class l**augh**.

aw = aw

awful	h**aw**
awning	j**aw**
br**aw**l	l**aw**
br**aw**n	l**aw**ful
c**aw**	l**aw**n
cl**aw**	p**aw**
cr**aw**	p**aw**n
d**aw**n	r**aw**
dr**aw**	s**aw**
dr**aw**er	scr**aw**l
f**aw**n	sh**aw**l
fl**aw**	squ**aw**k

Sentences
aw = aw

The **aw**ful br**aw**l of six br**aw**ns was a dr**aw** as number six's j**aw** was cracked and the l**aw** asserted that it was unl**aw**ful.

"C**aw**, c**aw**", it squ**aw**ked, lifting its cr**aw**, and I s**aw** its cl**aw** p**aw**ing the **aw**ning.

The fl**aw** in the plan is that r**aw** chicken is **aw**ful.

To catch the f**aw**n, h**aw** to the left and cross the l**aw**n.

At d**aw**n I shall dr**aw** an **aw**ful scr**aw**l on the top of F**aw**n's sh**aw**l.

Nip p**aw**ed the chess p**aw**n and it fell into the dr**aw**er.

ay = long a

astray	Murray
away	pay
bay	payment
clay	play
crayon	pray
day	ray
dismay	runway
essay	say
Fay	slay
fray	spray
gay	stay
gray	stray
hay	subway
holiday	Sunday
jay	sway
lay	tray
may	way
midday	

Sentences
ay = long a

Sunday at midday, stay to play a gay holiday.

Fay, Jay and Ray may play but stay away of the runway.

The bay is clay to his dismay, stray away.

On a gray day, do not dismay but stay and play with crayons, clay, and essays.

I say a sun's stray ray on Sunday may help him pray.

Lay the hay payment on the subway tray and stay away.

be = b + long ē

be
Beatrix
bebop
befit
before
began
beget
begin
begot
begun
behold
being
belong
beset
besot
beyond

Sentences
be = b + long ē

To **be**, or not to **be** is what was **be**ing discussed at the club.

At the **be**ginning, **be**fore I got there, they had **be**gun with **be**funding the club's bank.

Before I can get them to **be**long, **be**gin to get funding **be**yond costs.

Jim was **be**sot with **Be**atrix **be**fore **be**holding her at the club.

Being with him **be**gets a sensitivity of **be**longing and **be**ing **be**set with well**be**ing.

They listened to **be**bop and **be**gan to **be**get gladness **be**yond what they **be**held proper.

Behold, **be**yond the hill **be**gins the sunset.

Beware, the lamp is lit, and all must **be** here **be**fore his army **be**sets us.

ce #1 = s (silent e)

absence	lance
advance	notice
chance	novice
dance	office
distance	officer
disturbance	palace
dunce	pence
entrance	practice
face	prance
fence	presence
force	prince
glance	riddance
importance	sentence
justice	trance

Sentences
ce #1 = s (silent e)

Novices in trances in Vegas are dunces; it is the force of chance that controls the lance of luck.

The importance of the notice of no disturbance in the distance force is an advance in justice.

Advance to the fence of the palace dance entrance and glance at the face of the prince.

The absence and riddance of the presence of that dunce at practice gives us a chance to advance.

The officer's notice at his office of the disturbance in the force will bring an advance sentence.

ce #2 =se

accept
celebrant
celebrity
celery
cell
Celt
Celtic
cemetery
centipede
censor
census
cent
center
central

ceramics
certificate
cervix
December
excel
excellent
eccentric
except
Frances
necessity
princess
success
successful

Sentences
ce #2 =se

The necessity, princess, is in accepting that a celebrity is necessary for the successful December celebrity center.

Except for eccentric Frances, the certificate for excellence in ceramics will be given to the Celtic Central Center.

The necessity is in having a successful census of the number of cells in the center by December.

Accept not a cent to be the celebrant in the celebrity celebrating event.

Pick celery next to the cement walk except next to the cemetery.

A centipede excels in successfully squirming in an eccentric manner.

ce #3 =se + long e

cedilla   Cedric
cede   intercede
cement

Sentences
ce #3 =se + long e

When interceded, Cedric ceded the cedilla mark on that word.

Cedric interceded in the cement stand.

ce #4 =sh

grocer   grocery

Sentences
ce #4 =sh

The grocer is in his grocery.

cean = shun

crustacean   cean

Sentences
cean = shun

Crustaceans exist in oceans.

cei = s + long ē

deceive   receivable
receipt   receive

Sentences
cei = s + long ē

Do not deceive, stock the receipts in the receivables desk.

ch #1 = ch

bench	chilly	finch
branch	chin	hunch
brunch	chink	inch
bunch	chintz	lichen
Chad	chip	linchpin
chaffinch	chipmunk	lunch
champ	chit	much
chant	chock	munch
chap	chop	ostrich
chasm	chubby	pinch
chat	chug	punch
check	chum	ranch
cherry	chunk	rich
chess	conch	sandwich
chest	crunch	scrunch
chestnut	drench	such
chick	duchess	trench
children	enchantment	winch
chill	French	

Sentences
ch #1 = ch

The **ch**ubby Fren**ch** **ch**ildren sit on a ran**ch** ben**ch** and mun**ch** and crun**ch** a ri**ch** lun**ch**.

A **ch**affin**ch** sat on a bun**ch** of bran**ch**es and sang to the en**ch**antment of a **ch**ipmunk.

An ostri**ch** **ch**ick pin**ch**ed a **ch**ap and ran to the **ch**ildren in the **ch**asm tren**ch**.

Ri**ch**ard's **ch**icken sandwi**ch** and **ch**illy **ch**erry pun**ch** ends his **ch**ildren's brun**ch**.

The **ch**amp boxer's pun**ch** on that **ch**ap's **ch**in was su**ch** a **ch**eck in his bank.

Win**ch** up the **ch**est **ch**ock full of **ch**ips of ri**ch** gōld and fix it with a lin**ch**pin.

Can a **ch**ipmunk **ch**op bran**ch**es into **ch**ips?

I had a hun**ch** that dren**ch**ed his fun.

The Dut**ch** du**ch**ess in **ch**intz can win at **ch**ess.

ch #2 = k

chaos
chemo
chord
choreography **(ph=f)**
chorus
chorister
chromo
Chris
Chrīst
chrīster
Christmas

chromosome
chronic
chronicle
chronology
chronometer
chrysōlite (y=ī)
chrysalis (y=ī)
chrome
chromium
chrōmatic

Sentences
ch #2 = k

At **Ch**ristmas all the **ch**oristers of the **ch**ōrus sing songs of the nativity of **Ch**rist.

The **ch**oreōgraphy of each **ch**ord is a wonderful **ch**ronicle of **Ch**ristmas.

The **ch**ronōlogy of **Ch**rist has its origin in a **ch**ronic trust in His proverbs.

Chris was **ch**ristened at **Ch**ristmas.

A **ch**rysalis has a **ch**rōmatic insect within.

That is a disorder in the **ch**ronic order of things.

Chris got well with **ch**emotherapy.

Chris' **ch**rōmosomes were not assessed on a **ch**rōnometer.

Chrōme and **ch**rōmium are metallic.

ci #1 = sh

ancient
especial
especially
special
specially

Sentences
ci #1 = sh

That ancient man especially brings special gifts that will specially charm a special King.

That ancient man is special, especially for Tom.

Two Alphabets- Phonogram In Contrasting Color

A Practical Guide to Phonics

ci #2 = si

acid
accident
cigar
cinder
Cinderella
cinema
citizen
citric
citrus
city
civet
civic
codicil
Francis
glancing
incident
pencil
rescind

Sentences
ci #2 = si

The incident of the acid accident involved citric acid.

The civic codicil rescinded the citizen's help to the city.

The incident of the accident to the city cinema rescinds all civic help.

The black cigar cinder marked the codicil as well as if a pencil.

The accident did not stop Francis's glancing at the citizens.

Cinderella is at the city cinema to help all citizens.

Vitamin C is from citrus and is better than penicillin.

ci #3 = s + long ī

cider	decided
cite	recital
exciting	scientific
excitement	scientist

Sentences
ci #3 = s + long ī

At lunch the scientist decide to cite his exciting scientific recital.

Then that decided scientist recited his exciting scientific discovery.

The scientific academics excitedly cited the scientist's recital of his discovery.

The excited scientists decided to drink cider as they cited him.

The scientists' excitement lasted as long as the recital and the cider.

cious = shus

deli**cious**
pre**cious**
vi**cious**

Sentences
cious = shus

Meg is deli**cious** and pre**cious** but vi**cious**.

The dinner was deli**cious** with pre**cious** silver dishes.

Gollum vi**cious**ly called his ring his pre**cious** and that it was deli**cious**.

The king combated with vi**cious** battles for Gollum's pre**cious** ring.

cir = sr

circle	circumspect
circlet	circumvent
circum-	circus
circumflex	circumference

Sentences
cir = sr

The **circumference** of that **circle** is **circumspect**.

Circle the **circumference** of the **circus** land, it's **circumspect**.

To **circumvent** that **circus** artist the gang had to **circle** all the **circumference** of the **circus**.

This **circlet** is bigger than the king's **circlet**. The king has on his family **circlet**.

Circumflex and **circum** are difficult to understand.

Circumflex has to do with accents on syllables.

Circum is the first part of **circumvent**.

co = cu

color	confess
colorless	connect
command	consent
company	consult

Sentences

co = cu

Consult the color of the company command flag, it's colorless.

That printing company confessed that they did not have the consent to print colorless flags.

Sam consulted his company and they commanded that company to print the flags in color.

Sam connected to the company's command and they consented to print the flags in color.

ct

act
actress
cactus
collect
collecting
director
exactly
expect
fact
insect
object
October
reflect
reflector
suspect

Sentences
ct

The man shifting the reflect or lamp suspected that the actress was not acting exactly as the director expected.

That director expects the actress to act exactly as directed.

The actress objected to his comment and also that the director thinks that her acting is not better.

That actress collects cactus plants and suspected the cactus were not well kept as they had insects.

In October, the club for collecting insects collected six hundred insects suspected of biting cactus.

They reflected on the fact that cactus are expected to be taller.

cu = ceu

accuse
cue
Hercules
occupy
rescue
ridicule
Mercury

Sentences

cu = ceu

Hercules accused Mercury of not rescuing on cue.

Mercury ridiculed Hercules of occupying himself with ridiculous rescues.

On cue, Hercules accused Mercury of being ridiculous.

Mercury hit Hercules with a billiard cue.

cy #1 = s + long ē

chancy
Clancy
clemency
fancy
lacy
Macy
Mercy
Nancy
Yancy

Sentences

cy #1 = s + long ē

Clancy's chancy fancy for Nancy begs for clemency.

Yancy wants a lacy dress from Macys.

Clemency and mercy are best for mankind.

cy #2 = si

bi**cy**cle
cycle (si & sī)
cyclic
cygne
Cygnus
cylinder
cylindrical
cymbal
cynic
cynical
Cynthia
cyst

Sentences
cy #2 = si

That **cy**nical **cy**nic will not help him on his bi**cy**cle.

That small **cy**gnet got stuck in a **cy**linder in the **cy**clic fall term.

The **cy**mbal crashed and the **cy**nic jumped. The swelling on his leg was a **cy**st.

That **cy**nic will be **cy**nical if asked of the **cy**mbalist's **cy**st.

A **cy**linder is a **cy**lindrical object.

Cygnus the swan is a set of stars.

cy #3 = s + long ī

cyanic
cybernetics
cycad
cycle (si & sī)
cyclic (si & sī)
cyclist
cyclamen
cyclotron
Cyprus
Cypress
cytoplasm

Sentences
cy #3 = s + long ī

The **cy**clamen has buds but the **cy**cad is a fern.

A Mexican **cy**press has the largest trunk in the world.

Consider studying **cy**bernetics and the **cy**clic **cy**cles of the **cy**clotron.

The **cy**toplasm is part of the cell.

Cyclic and **cy**clic sound both s+short i and s+long ī.

A **cy**bernetics expert cannot **cy**cle under a **cy**press as fast as an atom in a **cy**cle.

The **cy**clist fell off his **cy**cle in **Cy**prus.

de = d + long ē

decap
defect
demand
desist
depart
depress
desert

Sentences
de = d + long ē

Under **de**mand, **de**part and **de**sist from **de**manding to **de**fect.

Ned, **de**scend and **de**fect.

When Dirk **de**fected, **de**pressed, he **de**parted and did **de**scend into darkness.

Desist and do not **de**fect as the next step **de**caps **de**pression.

Dirk felt **de**pressed and did not **de**sist **de**serting his land so **de**parted.

A part of a **de**pression in the land was his and he **de**serted it.

dge = j

badge	judgment
badger	ledge
bridge	ledger
Bridget	lodge
budge	midge
dredge	midget
dodge	pledge
edge	porridge
fidget	Rodger
fledgeling	sledge
fudge	smudge
grudge	wedge
hedge	trudge
hedgehog	
judge	

Sentences
dge = j

In the ledger the artful dodger pledged to have porridge without a grudge.

He jumped the hedge and fell on a fidgeting hedgehog and a midget badger.

Bridget's badger will not budge from under the bridge; he fidgets and fudges and calls on the hedgehog in his lodge under the hedge.

In the judge's judgment did Rodger win his fledge badge with his pledge to help dredge the edge of the bridge?

His better judgment tells him to dodge the dredge on the bridge's edge.

The midget had a wedge to push the edge of the sledge out of the sludge and then trudged to Midge's lodge.

The badge got smudged on the edge when the ledge slipped and Bridget fell in the sludge.

Rodger sells fudge from the sledge on the bridge and Bridget sells fudge at the lodge.

di = d + long ī

diagram
dining
direct
directly

Sentences
di = d + long ī

Bob sketched the **di**agram **di**rectly on the plank on which we were **di**ning.

The **di**rect form Bob sketched for Bill was a perfect **di**agram.

e #1 = long ē

be	Felix
began	he
begun	heroic
belong	immediate
beyond	Jesse
deliver	length
demand	me
depart	reluctantly
depend	remember
deserve	request
desist	reward
determined	secret
eject	she
equipment	we
eternal	zebra

Sentences
e #1 = long ē

He, she, it, we, and me belong to pronouns.

Reluctantly I remember the verb "to be" and the verbs that belong and depend on it.

Felix's request that Jesse deserved to get an immediate secret reward began a demand beyond his desire.

He was determined to deliver the equipment to me before we had begun to depart.

She ejected the disk and ran the length of the program before the electric demand crashed the equipment.

To be or not to be: that is if we exist, do not desist, and belong to an eternal being.

He had a zebra we depended on Felix to deliver with a request to be elected and not rejected as secret zebra deliverer.

e #2 = short e

despondent	elope
electric	enemy
electrify	erect
electrode	erupt
electron	pretty
eleven	relate

Sentences
e #2 = short e

He was despondent after his enemy eloped with his pretty friend.

Electrify the electric industry and relate and tell them of the erupting of his eleven electrodes.

Erect an electron apparatus that will pretty well corner the electric market.

But do not be despondent if the enemy gets there first with his eleven erupting electrodes and wins a market.

e #3 = silent e

addictive	horseback
adjective	live
been	nonsense
captive	nurse
cerve	olive
else	opposite
examine	promise
favorite	purse
forgive	sense
give	serve
glimpse	solve
gone	twelve
have	verse
horse	

Sentences
e #3 = silent e

Nonsense nurse, it's addictive, I live on horseback.

Promise to examine his twelve favorite horses or else.

There is no adjective that can even give a glimpse of that purse-winning horse but a verse can.

Forgive me as I have gone and lost my senses when thinking of that horse.

After he had been captured and held captive, he was let go as he did give them an olive branch and his horse.

Serve him the opposite of what he asks to solve his addictive problem.

e_e = long ē_e

breve	even
Chinese	evening
complete	impede
delete	here
Eden	Japanese
eject	mere
eke	meter
elect	millipede
electric	Pekinese
electrify	Pete
electron	precede
eleven	Steve
eve	

Sentences
e_e = long ē_e

Elect Steven to completely electrify the Chinese and Japanese this evening.

Pete, delete the eleven disks and eject even Steven's.

On this sixth evening, the Chinese completely electrify the public.

A mere eleven millipedes = a meter.

To impede an electron is to completely delete it.

Here, even Eden in the evening is electrifying.

Delete six meters and precede to complete the Japanese electric meters.

A breve on top of ă, ĕ, ĭ, ŏ, ŭ, means short vowel.

A micron on top of ā, ē, ī, ō, ū, means long vowel.

Eke a complete evening from eleven seconds.

ea #1 = long ē (silent a)

appeal	east	meaning
appear	Easter	meat
beach	eat	near
bead	flea	neat
beak	fear	pea
beaker	feast	peacock
bean	freak	read
beast	gear	real
beat	gleam	ream
clean	hear	peak
clear	heat	squeak
cream	Jean	peach
deal	least	peanut
dean	lease	peat
dear	jeans	please
dream	leader	reach
each	leaf	reap
eager	leak	scream
eagle	leap	sea
easel	meal	seal

Sentences
ea #1 = long ē (silent a)

The near peat bog was hit by at least six streaks and it appears he lost his hearing.

The eager beaver squealed when the mean weasel feasted on his treat.

A weasel is not a mean freak as the meaning of freak is not real.

Please teach Jean to sip tea and eat a cream treat in the heat of the east beach.

Please, release each eager eagle to reach the nearest peak and feast on meat.

Dean, at least beam up the team to beat off each fearful beast.

Seat the seal near the beach and appear to hear the sea speak.

The dean appeared eager to eat the lean meat feast.

I fear eating a peaches and cream treat is not a feast for each weakling.

ea #2 = long ā

break
breaks
great
breaking
breaker

Sentences
ea #2 = long ā

Suddenly, a great breaker breaks on him, breaking his leg.

It was a great sport break for him but breaking his leg was bad.

ea #3 = silent a

bedstead	instead
breast	lead
bread	meant
breakfast	measure
breath	read
dead	ready
deaf	spread
death	steady
dreadful	sweat
dread	sweater
feather	thread
head	tread
health	wealth
heather	weapon
heavier	weather
heavy	

Sentences
ea #3 = silent a

I read my log and instead am ready for breakfast so will spread my bread with jam.

I meant to spread the breakfast bread, instead I read with dread of his death.

I dread the dreadful heavy breath spread from the head of my bedstead and sweat as if death had patted my head.

Instead of measuring his health, that deaf man has it in his head to be ready for death.

The healthier thing for him to do is to measure all of his wealth and steadily do healthy things as run on a treadmill.

Having a feather quilt is healthy.

The breath of living is having read a lot.

He wants to have ready heavy sweaters for when he sweats and gasps for breath in bad weather.

Chicken breasts for breakfast and the steady measure of all the butter he spreads on his bread will help.

Sentences
ea #3 = silent a (cont...)

He reads in dreadful weather and is ready on the plot's thread.

Do not pick up heavy lead things as our legs are not meant to hold up heavy leaden objects.

Most important for health, do not go where there are heavy weapons.

ea #4 = long ēā

cr**ea**tive
cr**ea**te

Sentences
ea #4 = long ēā

That cr**ea**tive man cr**ea**tes stunning successes with no effort.

Cr**ea**te cr**ea**tivity.

ear #1 = long ē + r

app**ear**	h**ear**
d**ear**	n**ear**
dr**ear**y	t**ear**s
ear	w**ear**y
f**ear**	w**ear**ily

Sentences
ear #1 = long ē + r

I f**ear** to h**ear** of Ned's dr**ear**y n**ear**ness to Tom's w**ear**y t**ear**s.

It app**ear**s that when Tom's d**ear**est Jan h**ear**s Ned's dr**ear**y gossip, she'll think he did it.

W**ear**ily he went in t**ear**s to be n**ear** her and offer her costly **ear**rings.

When he hung them on her **ear**s, in t**ear**s Jan got n**ear**er to him and app**ear**ed happy.

Ned's t**ear**s stopped and he hugged Jan n**ear** and called her d**ear**.

ear #2 = âr

bear
pear
swear
tear
wear

Sentences
ear #2 = âr

I sw**ear** that b**ear** t**ear**s skin.

Do not t**ear** the pants he w**ear**s to pick p**ear**s.

ear #3 = er

earl
earn
earth
heard
learn

learned
learning
pearl
search
yearn

Sentences
ear #3 = er

I heard that early men yearned to search the earth and earn the pearls of learning.

He can search but learning is earned not just searched or yearned.

A pearl of learning is better than a hundred strings of pearls.

ear #4 = ar

heart
hearth

Sentences
ear #4 = ar

Bev's hearth is heart-full of warmth.

The heart of a hot heart brings gladness to the heart.

The heart of a kid rings in his heartstrings.

eau = ea

beautiful
beauty

Sentences
eau = ea

A beautiful sunset is blissful beauty.

A thing of beauty brings a beautiful joy.

ed #1 = d

bagg**ed**
bang**ed**
begg**ed**
cal**led**
chil**led**
chinn**ed**
farm**ed**
fel**led**
flagg**ed**
gather**ed**
liv**ed**
pegg**ed**
penn**ed**
pinn**ed**
rush**ed**
wing**ed**

Sentences
ed #1 = d

I liv**ed** and begg**ed** and gather**ed** and farm**ed** and call**ed** on God.

Baggins call**ed** the Hobbits and begg**ed** the men gather**ed** to club the wing**ed** dragon until fell**ed** and bagg**ed**.

I bagg**ed** a wing**ed** robin, flagg**ed** his leg and penn**ed** his number on a list.

Jim pull**ed** with his hands, chinn**ed** himself up and bang**ed** his chin on a fell**ed** branch.

I penn**ed** a letter to Rob and gather**ed** his address from where Peg liv**ed**.

I chill**ed** and call**ed** the gang gather**ed** in Jeb's liv**ed**-in pad with posters pinn**ed** on the walls.

ed #2 = id

bat**ted**
band**ed**
hand**ed**
land**ed**
net**ted**
pant**ed**
part**ed**
pat**ted**
pet**ted**
plant**ed**
print**ed**
rest**ed**
visit**ed**
want**ed**
wind**ed**

Sentences
ed #2 = id

I batted left-handed and planted it in his wanted banded target.

I panted and rested but wanted to get the netted winded minx.

I wanted it to be printed and handed to him at six.

Meg patted and petted a banded egret as winded Nip panted and rested.

Dad printed left-handed a gilded text and handed it to the post man.

Sam and Ned visited the pond and netted and landed ten banded fish.

Ned parted after Jim visited him and planted ten printed tags on his plants.

Ann rested but printed a letter to Ted as Sam wanted him after Ted visited Peg.

ed #3 = t

asked
barked
clipped
cracked
dressed
dripped
finished
fixed
flapped
hatched
hopped
husked
jumped
marked
missed

napped
scratched
skipped
stacked
scrapped
parked
pecked
promised
stuffed
slapped
whipped
thanked
tripped

Sentences
ed #3 = t

I hopped and jumped and skipped and tripped and missed a packed stacked box.

I stopped and stepped and trapped a marked skunk.

The pink mink barked and hopped and dripped and picked a fixed marked box.

Nip scratched and barked and the trapped chick flapped his wings and pecked him.

Ann clipped a stuffed dog, stitched it, and so finished Pat's promised gift.

Sam asked if Ned thanked Ann for Nip's gift.

Sam fixed the cracked pan as it dripped and Ann slipped on the drops.

Ned tripped on Nip but never whipped him. Ann dressed but missed the promised trip.

The chick hatched and hopped from the cracked egg.

ee = long ē

agree	flee	reed	steel
agreement	fleet	screen	steep
bee	free	see	street
beef	glee	seed	tee-hee
beet	green	seek	teepee
bleed	heel	seem	teeth
coffee	indeed	seen	three
creek	jeep	seventeen	tree
creep	jeer	sheep	tweet
deed	keel	sheet	weed
deep	keep	sixteen	week
eel	need	sleek	weep
feed	peel	sleep	yippee
feel	peep	sleet	
feet	peer	speed	
fifteen	queen	steed	

Sentences
ee = long ē

I creep up the tree to seek seventeen peepers and tweeters.

See sixteen sleek sheep deep asleep fifteen feet from the three green trees.

With a queer cheer, yippee, jeer the beery leering steering creep.

See the jeep speed fifteen feet into the reed weeds of the deepest creek.

Indeed, I agree, seek to keep the fee, the agreement, the seventeen sheets of the deed, and speedily flee

Feed the sleek eel beef and peer from the keel to seek to freeze his teeth.

Tee-hee, can Hal creep up and feel a bee in the deep green reeds and keep his speed?

The queen is weeping as the kingdom needs three swift steeds this week.

eer = long ē + r

beer	neer-do-well
cheer	queer
deer	seer
jeer	steer
leer	

Sentences
eer = long ē + r

In the b**eer** hall there was a d**eer** hanging on the wall.

A **seer** was sitting with a n**eer**-do-well that was bumming a b**eer**

The b**eer** barman j**eer**ed at the qu**eer** l**eer** of that n**eer**-do-well.

The men there ch**eer**ed the barman and st**eer**ed the bum out.

The **seer** with the qu**eer** gawk did not ch**eer** and called them to stop or turn into d**eer**.

The **seer** thinks that a d**eer** can be hit with bad st**eer**ing.

ei #1 = long ā

beige
feint
rein
reign
skein
veil

Sentences
ei #1 = long ā

The joker made a feint at the king's reign.

All his men dressed in beige and reined in to go into the fortress.

Then they crept inside the hall to the king's veiled bed.

But the king's men trapped them and rolled a beige skein about them.

ei #2 = long ē

ceil
ceiling
either
Keith
Neil
Neither
seize

Sentences
ei #2 = long ē

Do not seize either Keith or Neil for neither has it.

Neither Keith nor Neil nor either Ceil seized the ceiling lamp.

eigh = long ā

bob-sleigh
eighty
freight
neigh
weigh
weight
weighing

Sentences
eigh = long ā

The **weight** of **eight** **freight**s is **weigh**ty, **neigh**bor.

Eighty **bob-sleigh** animals all **neigh**ing is bad for **neigh**bors.

eign #1 = in

foreign
sovereign

Sentences
eign #1 = in

Rex is the sovereign King of a foreign land.

eign #2 = long ā + n

feign
reign

Sentences
eign #2 = long ā + n

Feign happiness when the reigning king steps in.

eir #1 = long ē

weird
weir

Sentences
eir #1 = long ē

With a weird yell the dragons landed in the weir.

eir #2 = âr

heir
their
heirloom

Sentences
eir #2 = âr

Their heir grasps the heirloom pin and ends the unjust plot.

el = ul

barrel	shellac
bevel	swivel
camel	travel
chisel	intellect
hazel	marvel
model	tunnel
nickel	Wendell

Sentences
el = ul

With a chisel, bevel the log, cut it into a barrel and rub shellac on it.

Wendell traveled on a camel into the dark tunnel.

I wish for Hāzel's intellect.

Marvel comics do not help his intellect.

A barrel can swivel and spin and roll back to Wendell.

A nickel will not go far to find seven marvels. Hazel put his nickels in a piggy bank.

eo = long ē

people
hideous

Sentences
eo = long ē

Hideous people do not act as hideous people within.

Do not act as if those people are hideous, they are not.

A monster may be hideous but not act hideous.

er #1 = r

after	flickers	otter
aftermath	germ	pepper
Albert	hammer	perfect
banner	hanger	perhaps
batter	hamper	rafter
Bert	hamster	river
better	helper	Robert
bigger	her	rocker
bitter	herd	scamper
blinkers	Herbert	pert
blister	hunger	Peter
bother	interest	September
butter	jerk	serpent
clatter	lantern	silver
clerk	letters	sister
clever	liberty	slipper
dagger	lobster	stern
Dexter	manners	summer
differ	matter	supper
dinner	member	tern
duster	merit	trigger
enter	mister	under
Ernest	mixer	verb
ever	never	very
fern	November	western
finger	number	winter

Sentences
er #1 = r

Her helper Herbert had a number of different blisters under his fingers.

After a perfect summer, September, October, November and December scampered into winter.

The merit of the scampering river otters and the pert summer terns is being very clever to not bother over the bitter winters.

Bert is a better batter, is a clever mixer, never has bad manners and is perhaps a perfect rocker.

Mister Peter never ever bothered to get bigger silver slippers for his sister Roberta.

For supper, Mister Peter Piper picked perhaps a perfect peck of pickled peppers.

er #2 = long ē + r

serial   period   material

Sentences
er #2 = long ē + r

This serial will form material for a period film.

ere #1 = long ē + r

adhere   merely   serial
here   severe   sincere

Sentences
ere #1 = long ē + r

Merely adhere a print of the serial here.

Be sincere and merely adhere severely to his family.

ere #2 = â + r

somewhere   where
there   whereupon
therefore

Sentences
ere #2 = â + r

Therefore and whereupon: where is there? Somewhere?

es = z

people
hideous

Sentences
es = z

Elves can run fast up rock shelves.

Rock shelves are effortless for elves

eu = eu

Europe   Neuter

Sentences
eu = eu

Europe is not neuter.

eve = long ē + v
(silent e) (rule ē _e)

Eve
grieve
evening

Sentences
eve = long ē + v

That evening Eve grieved for him.

I grieved with Eve all evening.

To grieve is natural but sad.

ew = eu

blew	grew	newt
crew	hew	pew
chew	jewel	screw
drew	Matthew	skewer
ewer	mews	stew
few	new	threw
flew	news	

Sentences

ew = eu

A few men flew Matthew into the mews.

The crew threw a new jewel into the pew.

Chew the stew and drink from the ewer.

The wind blew the news and it flew into Saint Matthew's pew.

I drew the newt that grew into that monster.

Few chew that rubber jewel on the skewer.

ey #1 = long ē

abb**ey**	k**ey**
all**ey**	medl**ey**
Berkl**ey**	pull**ey**
Beverl**ey**	Rodn**ey**
chimn**ey**	Sidn**ey**
donk**ey**	Stanl**ey**
Dudl**ey**	troll**ey**
Harv**ey**	turk**ey**
hock**ey**	vall**ey**
Humphr**ey**	voll**ey**
Jeffr**ey**	Westl**ey**
jock**ey**	

Sentences
ey #1 = long ē

Beverley and Berkeley went to Westley Abbey in the valley.

In 1840, the chimney of the abbey was the target of a volley from Humphrey Jeffrey's guns.

There in the alley they met the grand jockey, Sidney Stanley and his donkey.

The jockey did a medley of hockey hits on his donkey.

Rodney thinks that the key to pulling that trolley is to get a pulley for the donkey.

Harry thinks Dudley is a turkey.

ey #2 = ā

grey
obey
prey
they
whey

Sentence
ey #2 = ā

They did not obey and on that grey morn they fell prey to a monster.

Then they had curds and whey for dinner.

eyre = âr + long ē
ir + long ē

Eyre
Eyrie

Sentences
eyre = âr + long ē
ir + long ē

The lawyer went on his **eyre** and passed the tallest **eyrie**.

g = j

gel
gelid
gem
gender
gēnius
gently
gēometry
germ
gibber
gin
gist
origin
vigil

Sentences
g =j

Gently the huge gēnius gibbered the gist of gēometry.

(note: geometry can also be pronounced with a silent e. g-ometry.)

The vigil was long and in the gelid wind the drinks gelled as if refrigerāted.

What gender was the origin of gems?

Think about gently putting the germs in the gel.

The plan is to have that gēnius gently cut the gems.

The gist of the matter is that gēometry is for all gēniuses.

To gibber is not for gēniuses.

Gin is a drink best served gelid.

ge = j

barge	large
barrage	larger
charge	leger
fidget	legend
forge	messenger
gelatin	nitrogen
general	orange
Genesis	page
gent	plunge
gently	ranger
George	refrigerate
gorge	sarge
hinge	sponge
huge	suggest
judgment	

Sentences
ge =j

General George suggested to the messenger on the barge that they first send the huge barrage and then charge.

The blacksmith forged a larger hinge and then plunged it into a wet sponge.

Orange gelatin is gently refrigerāted but not with nītrogen.

In Genesis the first pages begin the largest ledger of mankind.

When Gentle George is hot they refrigerāte him with a chilly wet sponge.

Sarge, do not fidget but send the ranger into the gorge to get the lost gent.

The ranger sent a messenger to the General that the lost gent was not in the gorge.

The gent was not lost but was on the barge nibbling orange gelatin.

gi = ji

engine (silent e)
frigid
gib
giblet
gin
giraffe (silent e)
imagine (silent e)
magic
region
regiment
rigid
Virgil

Sentences
gi =ji

Imagine the magic of visiting the historic rēgions of Virgil.

The **gist** of it all was that in the **frigid** winter the plants went **rigid**.

If in a deck; **gin** is fun, **gin** in a jug is drunk, or if it is an **engine**, it can fix cotton.

Imagine a rigid frigid engine carting **gin** for the rēgion's regiment.

Imagine a Thanksgiving turkey without **giblet** gravy.

Imagine the magic of a rēgion with **giraffes**.

I am in the rēgion of the rigid vigil of the sixth regiment.

Imagine Dante and Virgil on a magic trip.

gn =gn (silent g)

design
gnarl
gnat
gnaw (nå)
gnu
gnome
resign
sīgn

Sentences
gn =gn (silent g)

Desīgn me a habitat with no gnats.

The gnome desīgned me a desk with gnarled lumber.

I'm resīgned to that dog's gnawing the lot.

Sīgn or resīgn the desīgn.

gth = silent g + th

length　　　strength

Sentences
gth = silent g + th

His stren**gth** is in the len**gth** of his legs.

It is mental stren**gth** that prolongs the len**gth** of his living well.

The len**gth** of that marathon will call for vast stren**gth**.

Cut less len**gth** to get stren**gth**.

gue = g

analo**gue**
bro**gue**
decalo**gue**
demago**gue**
dialogue
epilo**gue**
fati**gue**
intri**gue**
monologue
mor**gue**
pedago**gue**
pla**gue**
prologue
rogue
travelo**gue**
vā**gue**

Sentences
gue = g

Analogue is the best magazine. Intrigue with pedagogues is common.

The rōgue's decalogue and dīalogue in brogue fatigues that demagogue.

His talk was so vāgue the demagogue left.

His brōgue is so strong that it is as a monolōgue.

The intrigue is where that rōgue is from.

The prōlogue to his travelogue is vāgue.

The epilogue to his plāgue is that he ended up in the morgue.

Intrigue with pedagogues is common.

gy = ji

apolo**gy**
gym
gymnasium
gymnastics
gymnast
gypsum
gyp
gypsy

Sentences
gy = ji

Gymnastics is best in a **gy**mnāsium.

I ask an apolo**gy** for the **gy**psy **gy**mnast at that **gy**mnāsium.

The **gy**psy did not **gy**p him when selling him that **gy**psum.

The **gy**psy's wagon brings him from **gy**mnāsium to **gy**mnāsium.

That **gy**psy wins in all the **gy**mnastics contests.

I go to the **gy**m but I am not a **gy**mnast.

silent h

Afghan
dishonest
dinghy
ghastly
ghost
honest
honesty
honor
John
school
shepherd
shepherdess
Thomas

Sentences
silent h

John served with **h**onor in Afg**h**anistan and his **h**onesty brings him **h**onor.

But T**h**omas was dis**h**onest in sc**h**ool and carried dis**h**onor to his family.

He robbed an afg**h**an and told the class that John was the robber.

A man's **h**onor is his most **h**onest gift and cannot just be gotten.

The s**h**epherd and s**h**epherdess watched the flocks and spotted the star.

Honestly, the g**h**astly g**h**ost was on the ding**h**y and drifted on.

The g**h**ōstly ding**h**y drifted past the dock and all yelled and ran.

i #1 = long ī

admiring	hind	rewind
advised	hiring	shiny
arrived	hired	silent
Bible	Inez	spider
bind	Iris	striking
blind	iron	tiger
child	ivy	tiny
dining	kind	triangle
direct	microscopic	trident
directly	mild	unkind
driver	mind	whined
find	pint	wild
grind	quiet	wind
hiding	rider	wives
hi	rind	

Sentences
i #1 = long ī

Fiery striking tiger hiding in the silent wild, find kindness.

The child with the black īris arrived directly to find blind Inez hiding.

Grīnd with iron and find tiny microscopic rinds.

I advised the admiring wives to not be directly unkīnd.

The wild wind whined in the ivy as it arrived.

I hired a driver and was hiring a rider to drive directly to the quiet Bible camp.

i #2 = long ē

Aline
Ali
dutiful
merriment
ugliness

Sentences
i #1 = long ē

Ali, forget ugliness; dutifulness and merriment is best to help Sebastian and Aline.

i #3 = u

April
denim
devil
sensible

Sentences
i #3 = u

A denim dress is devilishly sensible in April.

It is sensible to have six denim dresses as this April is devilishly hot.

Denim caps are alsō sensible for this hot April.

Denim was sensible for gōld diggers in devilishly hot sand banks

ice #1 = is

cowardice
Janice
practice

Sentences
ice #1 = is

Janice, do not practice cowardice.

But Janice thinks that cowardice cannot be practiced, it is there within a man.

Cowardice is an appalling mannerism and Janice watched Jim do it in gun practice.

In practice at the gun camp, his dog presented cowardice as well.

ice #2 = long ī + sz

advice	nice
dice	price
entice	rice
ice	slice
lice	spice
mice	twice

Sentences
ice #2 = long ī + sz

Jim's advice to Jack was to entice the mice with a nice cupful of rice.

Twice the mice did not smell the nice rice but the lice did.

Jack then enticed the mice with a slice of nice rice ice.

The spice of a tossing dice is a slice of fast living at a price.

ie #1 = long ē (silent ī)

belief	Jessie
believe	Leslie
brief	mischief
chief	priest
cutie	relief
fief	reprieve
field	shield
fiend	shriek
frieze	seize
grief	stories
hurried	thief
Jackie	yield
Jennie	

Sentences
ie #1 = long ē (silent ī)

The priest's belief in a shrieking fiend yielded little relief for chief Jackie.

Jessie's stories of believing that a thief hid in the field yielded a shriek from Leslie's friend.

Leslie's relief is that her friend Jessie's shriek was just mischief.

I believe that friend Jessie is a cutie.

ie #2 = long ī (silent e)

cried
die
dried
fie
fiery
fliers
fried
hie
dissatisfied
pliers
satisfied
tied
tried
pie
lie

Sentences
ie #2 = long ī (silent e)

I tried pliers to fix the fiery die but dissatisfied, let it lie.

Hie to the fiery dried logs if it is important to be satisfied.

After Ned's golf lie, dissatisfied Ben tried, then cried and cried.

"Fie", cried the monster as he tried to find hidden Jack to help him die.

I am satisfied with dried fried pumpkin pie.

The fliers tried to hold the tied wing with pliers where Jim lied but were dissatisfied.

Fiery gas fried the pumpkin pie.

i - e #3 = long ī_silent e

bike	lime	spike
bite	line	spider
bribe	live	spine
bride	Mike	spire
crime	mile	stile
despise	mine	strike
dime	Nile	stripe
dine	nine	strive
dive	pile	tile
drive	pine	time
entire	pipe	tire
fine	prime	twine
fire	prize	vine
five	ride	vise
hide	ripe	wide
hike	shine	wife
hive	shrive	wine
hire	side	wipe
kite	size	wire
life	slide	wives
like	smile	

Sentences
i - e #3 = long ī_silent e

The spider's bite spiked Mike's wife with nine lives.

Ride that bike and hide it in the pine pile aside of the wide drive, it's mine.

This time shrive with a wide smile and aspire to like life.

Despise dime bribes for every time it's a crime.

Drive a mile to the side of the prize pine and twine a vine with wire to fire your pride.

Smile and dine a bride with fine lime wine.

Wipe that tire in the vise and spin it five times on the entire line.

That fire will drive the hive to hide for their life.

Hike a mile, twine a kite and run.

ier = long ē + r

fierce
fiercely
pier
pierce
pierced
pierrot
tier

Sentences
ier = long ē + r

On the **pier** Jim **fiercely pierced Pierrot's** parrot.

The parrot had bitten him in a **fierce** attack.

They will bring the parrot to the vet to fix that **pierce**.

That **tier** 1 student's parrot is not as **fierce** as **Pierrot's**.

Can I get **pierced** next?

ies #1 = long īz

flies
lies
dies
ties

Sentences
ies #1 = long īz

Ben **ties** the net and **tries** to trap **flies** on the **pies**.

His **lies** will catch him if Ben **tries** to act as if he **dies** and acts so bad.

Ben **tries** and **lies** there and **dies** as part of the act.

Then he **flies** from the **pies** they toss at him.

ies #2 = ēz

armies
berries
bodies
candies
cookies
dollies
pennies
priest
puppies

Sentences
ies #2 = ēz

Strawberr**ies**, blackberr**ies**, raspberr**ies**, huckleberr**ies**, gooseberr**ies**, blueberr**ies**, and cranberr**ies**, are all berr**ies** but cherr**ies** and mulberr**ies** are not.

Coo**k**ies and cand**ies** on pretty little doll**ies** cost ten penn**ies**.

Both Bett**ies** had big baskets but the red basket had six pupp**ies** and the pink basket had seven baby doll**ies** and ten Barb**ies**.

The bod**ies** of the six pupp**ies** had fat little bell**ies**.

Arm**ies** march in big bod**ies** of men.

The pr**ies**t got coo**k**ies and cand**ies** and hundreds of penn**ies** to help the church.

igh = long ī

blight	lightning
bright	midnight
delightful	might
enlighten	nigh
fight	night
flight	plight
frighten	right
frightful	sigh
frightening	sight
high	slight
highness	tight
light	tighten
lighten	

Sentences
igh = long ī

The sentinel sighed, "That frightful midnight lightning last night might frighten his highness."

The right delightful night might brighten and enlighten his grand insight.

Fight that frightening blight as the farm's plight is nigh.

The fighter lightened boxes and his flight went higher and higher but then the boxes expanded a slight bit and tightened his lashings too tight.

The bright light from high lightened a delightful path to higher insight.

A delightful flight into the bright sunlight was not at all a slight plight in his sight.

ing = ing

acting	frosting	scrubbing
asking	gasping	scudding
banking	golfing	sending
blending	gulping	singing
blinking	hexing	slinging
boxing	hunting	spanking
bringing	inking	spending
bumping	insisting	splinting
busing	jumping	springing
clasping	king	standing
clinging	lending	stinging
drifting	mending	stocking
drinking	mixing	sudding
duckling	nixing	swinging
dumping	opting	taxing
dunking	ping	tempting
ending	printing	twisting
expecting	ringing	vexing
fixing	risking	waxing
flinging	rusting	winging

a	**e**	**i**
bagging	bedding	bidding
banning	begging	brimming
batting	betting	digging
canning	blending	dimming
cramming	getting	dipping
gabbing	helping	fibbing
jabbing	hemming	fitting
lagging	jetting	grinning
mapping	legging	hitting
nagging	netting	inning
passing	pegging	kidding
patting	penning	missing
sagging	petting	nipping
tagging	setting	pigging
tanning	vetting	pitting
tapping	webbing	ridding
wadding	wedding	ripping
yapping	wetting	skipping

		u
sin**ning**	jot**ting**	bud**ding**
sit**ting**	lob**bing**	bug**ging**
swim**ming**	log**ging**	but**ting**
tin**ning**	lop**ping**	club**bing**
tip**ping**	mop**ping**	cub**bing**
trim**ming**	pop**ping**	cut**ting**
win**ning**	pot**ting**	dub**bing**
yip**ping**	rob**bing**	gun**ning**
zip**ping**	rod**ding**	gut**ting**
	rot**ting**	hug**ging**
	sob**bing**	hum**ming**
o	sod**ding**	jut**ting**
blot**ting**	sop**ping**	log**ging**
bob**bing**	stop**ping**	mug**ging**
bog**ging**	top**ping**	pun**ning**
clop**ping**		rub**bing**
con**ning**		run**ning**
cop**ping**		lug**ging**
dot**ting**		sum**ming**
drop**ping**		sun**ning**
hog**ging**		tug**ging**
hop**ping**		
jog**ging**		

Sentences
ing = ing

Max is an act**ing**, vex**ing**, ragg**ing**, begg**ing**, fibb**ing**, robb**ing**, slugg**ing** man.

In golf**ing** the th**ing** in correct**ing** a sw**ing** is mend**ing** the ball if sw**inging**.

In winn**ing** at swimm**ing**, drift**ing**, dunk**ing**, and gulp**ing** will not help but slipp**ing** and gett**ing** sopp**ing** then act**ing** cunn**ing** is vex**ing**.

Hugg**ing**, humm**ing**, runn**ing**, sunn**ing**, napp**ing**, jogg**ing**, swimm**ing**, kidd**ing**, nibbl**ing**, grinn**ing** and act**ing** will help the k**ing** get well.

Blend**ing** box**ing** and drink**ing** is br**inging** him a quick end**ing**.

io = long īō

violet
violent

Sentences
io = long īō

Violet, do not be violent.

ious = long ē + us

furious
obvious
serious

Sentences
ious = long ē + us

I am serious, Dan is obviously furious.

It was obvious, Meg was serious but when Dan turned furious she sobbed.

ion = yun

accord**ion**
bill**ion**
compan**ion**
mill**ion**
opin**ion**
quadrill**ion**
trill**ion**

Sentences
ion = yun

I had a mill**ion**, then a bill**ion**, then a trill**ion** and then a quadrill**ion** but what I most want is a compan**ion**.

Jed's compan**ion** has opin**ion**s on a mill**ion**, bill**ion**, trill**ion** and quadrill**ion** things.

But in Jed's opin**ion**, his compan**ion** is better with an accord**ion**.

ir = r

astir	Kirk
bird	redbird
confirm	shirk
dirk	shirt
dirt	sir
dirty	skirt
fir	smirk
firm	stir
firmly	swirl
firn	third
first	thirsty
flirt	twirl
girl	whirlwind

Sentences
ir = r

The first girl's skirt swirls and twirls in the whirlwind.

The dirty slush is not firm firn.

Yes, sir, I confirm that I will plant the third fir in the dirt.

The redbird is astir with all the thirsty birds.

The third girl is first of all a flirt and smirks at Sir Kirk.

Do not shirk but stir out with firmness and get the dirk hidden in his shirt.

ire = long ī + r

admire	ire
aspire	mire
conspire	perspire
desire	retire
dire	respire
empire	sire
enquire	spire
esquire	squire
entire	tire
expire	tired
fire	umpire
inquire	wire
inspire	

Sentences
ire = long ī + r

That esquire did not desire to enquire as tired and will retire as thinks his admired sire will expire with ire.

Sire, inquire if your esquire aspires to conspire in the entire empire.

As the empire is mired in dire conspirers it will expire unless all do not tire but inspired, perspire to fix the sire's empire.

The fort's spires are on fire, get that admired squire to inspire all the tired esquires to expire the fire and wire the fort shut.

The bad esquire lost and the umpire will retire him from the fort.

ise = long ī + z

advise
criticize
surprise

Sentences
ise = long ī + z

Surprise, I advised Ron to criticize Tim.

In criticize, the "c" in cize is as "s" so it is as size.

jua = whä

Juan
Juanita
Tijuana

Sentences
jua = whä

Juan and Juanita went to Tijuana.

In Tijuana Juan and Juanita discovered the secret of the gilded ingots.

kn = n (silent k)

knell   knife   knock
knelt   knit   knoll
knick-knacks   knob   knot
knickers   knobless

Sentences
kn = n (silent k)

When he tripped, his knife fell from his knickers as he knocked his chin on the knobs of the knoll.

On the next knoll his partner Nell knelt knitting knobless knick-knacks.

Nell has a knack for knitting and knitted him a patch to go on the knot on his chin.

He lost his knife on that knoll and Nell went to pick it up and knot it back on his knickers.

Nell has a shelf full of knit knick-knacks that she knitted.

le = ul

ample	cripple	hobble
angle	crumble	horrible
ankle	cuddle	huddle
apple	dabble	humble
babble	dangle	invisible
baffle	dapple	jangle
battle	dazzle	jingle
bottle	dribble	juggle
bramble	example	jungle
brittle	fickle	kettle
bubble	fiddle	kittle
buckle	fumble	little
bundle	gabble	mantle
candle	giggle	mangle
cantle	gobble	meddle
cattle	grumble	muddle
cobble	guzzle	mingle
crackle	handle	mumble
crinkles	handlebar	muzzle
crinkle	heckle	

le = ul (cont...)

nettle	rumble	temple
nibble	saddle	terrible
nozzle	scrabble	tickle
nuzzle	scramble	tingle
paddle	scribble	tinkle
pebble	scrapple	tremble
pickle	scuttle	toddle
possible	settle	tumble
prickle	sickle	twinkle
problem	simple	uncle
puddle	single	visible
purple	sizzle	waddle
puzzle	shingle	waggle
raffle	snuggle	wangle
rattle	spindle	wiggle
rectangle	sprinkle	wobble
responsible	struggle	wrinkle
riddle	stumble	
ripple	tackle	
rubble	tangle	

Sentences
le = ul

Settle the little candle in the bottle in the middle of the purple mantle.

Scramble on the saddle and huddle the cattle that stumble, fumble and struggle in the horrible jungle.

A visible bubble can tickle and tinkle and vanish in a twinkle.

Wiggle, waggle and waddle and dazzle his little uncle.

Baffle the umpire with an example of his impossible dribbles.

mb = m (silent b)

bomb   limb   succumb
crumb   numb   thumb
dumb   plumb
lamb   plumber

Sentences
mb = m (silent b)

Thumbs up all to that plumber who stopped the bomb from going off.

That dumb terrorist held the bomb in his numb thumbs and the plumber grabbed it and tossed it in the river. That plumber's valor kept all from succumbing to the blast.

Not a crumb of brick fell.

A plumb did fall from a limb but that was all.

A lamb stepped on his numb thumb.

mn = m (silent n)

autumn
column
condemn
solemn
mnemonic
mneme

Sentences
mn = m (silent n)

In solemn autumn they condemned his mnemonic column.

Montessori's mneme is a sort of mnemonic memory.

In autumn his solemn thinking is part of his column on fall.

He penned his column and condemned the gunmen that horrified the land.

ng = ng

bang	hung	rang	sung
clang	long	sang	swung
fang	lung	song	tang
fungus	pang	sprang	tong
gong	pong	strong	Wong
hang	prong	stung	

Sentences
ng = ng

Bang and clang the gong and sing a song.

Mr. Wong swung his ping-pong bat with a strong hand.

That fungus in the tongs stung his lungs with a pang; hang it on that long prong.

The bell that he hung swung and rang a strong gong.

o #1 = long ō

alm**o**st	jell**o**	**o**pposite
als**o**	J**o**el	**o**sm**o**sis
banj**o**	leg**o**	**O**tt**o**
b**o**th	Mexic**o**	**o**ver
calic**o**	n**o**	**o**verfed
cr**o**cus	m**o**ment	**O**wen
cl**o**sing	m**o**st	Pedr**o**
d**o**n't	n**o**ble	p**o**em
fr**o**	N**o**el	p**o**et
fr**o**zen	N**o**vember	p**o**etry
g**o**	**O**ctober	p**o**st
gh**o**st	**o**men	p**o**stman
hell**o**	**o**mit	s**o**
h**o**-hum	**o**nly	st**o**ny
h**o**ping	**o**pen	w**o**n't
h**o**st		

Sentences
o #1 = long ō

No, Pedro won't go over the stony, frozen, ghostly land but also only noble Joel will go.

October and November in Mexico almost are the opposite of winter as with crocus and poetry both are almost Spring.

Opening his banjo, the calico cat sang to and fro hoping that Noel, his overfed host of the moment, also wanted his song.

Obeying his master and closing thē box of poems, Owen thē poet posted most of his omitted poems with thē postman.

Don't tell Otto "hello" when going "ho-hum" as most think it only a bad omen.

Most of his overfed fat form is not from jello nor from osmosis but from not omitting his frozen snacks.

o #2 = ôô

do
improve
improvement
into
losing
lose
move
prove
to
undo

Sentences
o #2 = ôô

Do undo that move to improve his plan and then move to lose it.

Do move to improve his chess movements to win not lose.

His moves prove Jim must improve into a champ.

Jim must undo his bad habits to do this big improvement.

Jim thinks he can do a lot to lose his bad moves to prove he can turn into a winner.

"Do improve Jim!" yell his pals, "Prove it to us and turn from losing into winning."

Jim improved so much that he did move from losing into winning, to prove to his pals their efforts helped him to improve.

o #3 = u

another	Errol	pardon
balcony	from	parrot
ballot	gallop	period
blossom	govern	person
bottom	grandmother	pistol
brother	handsome	polite
carrot	Harold	possess
chicory	hickory	purpose
command	impolite	prison
commit	kingdom	recognize
company	love	second
confess	melon	seldom
connect	mommy	shove
consent	Monday	some
consult	month	something
cover	mother	son
daffodil	nothing	wagon
discover	octopus	welcome (silent e)
dove	other	wisdom
dozen	oven	wonderful

Sentences
o #3 = u

Son, discover that with love and wisdom, Brother, Grandmother, and Mommy seldom commit impolite commands.

Among the blossoms in Anderson's wagon were some wonderful daffodils, a dozen carrots, melons, chicory and hickory

Another ballot Monday recognizes that polite Errol won and will govern the kingdom; second was handsome Harold.

Mother welcomed the other person's pardon as Harold's confession covered his purpose with the pistol in prison.

Nothing in this month's consultant's period connected something from his company's consented purpose.

o_e #1 = long ō_silent e

alone	elope	mote	smoke
bone	envelope	motel	spoke
broken	froze	nose	stone
choke	globe	note	stole
clove	grove	owe	store
code	hole	poke	stove
coke	home	pole	strobe
compote	hope	pope	stroke
cone	hormone	probe	tone
cope	hose	robe	tote
cove	hotel	rode	trove
dome	joke	Rome	vote
dope	joker	rope	woke
dote	Jones	rose	wove
dove	mole	rove	yoke
drove	mope	slope	

Sentences
o_e #1 = long ō_silent e

Vote with hope to help this broken globe.

Jones the joker drove alone to his hotel to note a joke he spoke.

Bones rode home to tote a coke and compote up the slope to the grove and elope with Rose.

The dope put the code in an envelope and hid it in the stove until the smoke woke him up.

A hole in the dome cone drove the dope to poke a pole up and probe for the code.

To cope with a broken bone he drove to Rome and spoke to the robed Pope.

The mole almost froze at his home in the hole next to the stone on the slope.

The dope stole a strobe stove from the motel store.

o_e #2 = u_silent e

come
cover
discover
done
honey
love
lovely
money
none
welcome

Sentences
o_e #2 = u_silent e

Honey, come and discover what a lovely welcome they had for us.

They have spent none of the money we sent to help them.

They tell us that Jim's money covered it all and the cover was done with love.

Jim discovered that love is more than money and that having no money but lots of love is best.

Talking to them, I thanked them for such a lovely welcome and will come in the morning.

This is so lovely, they all chipped in the money with love.

Thanks for the love, honey.

oa #1 = long ō

approach	foal	oak
board	foam	oar
boast	goal	oats
boat	goat	poach
coach	gloam	road
coal	groan	roam
coast	Joan	roast
coat	load	shoal
coax	loaf	soak
cockroach	loam	soap
cloak	loan	throat
croak	moat	toad
float	oaf	toast

Sentences
oa #1 = long ō

Joan, approach and toast the boasting, gloating coach, his oafs won a goal.

Get on board with an oar, open the moat, and float the boat to approach the shoal on the foaming coast.

Poach roasted oats to coax the coal black foal roaming the road.

Do not groan; lend the cloak to Joan, put on his soaked coat, and roam the oaks.

Soap the throat of that croaking toad.

The cockroach is in the loam: the goat is poaching a loaf.

oa #2 = ä

abroad   broad

Sentences
oa #2 = ä

When he went abroad his ticket was for a broad number of lands.

A man with a broad back is strong.

To go abroad is to go across the Atlantic.

oar = long ō + r

board
boar
cupboard
hoard
hoary
oars
roar
roaring
soaring

Sentences
oar = long ō + r

In the cupboard his hoary hoard of boar hams left a spent hint of insipid squid.

In the rear the roaring hoary boar attacked Jim´s men by soaring on top of them.

His men grabbed the oars and fled the roaring boar.

Ned called the all aboard as the ship soared into the wind.

oe = long ō

doe
foe
goes
hoe
oboe
roe
sloe
toe
woe

Sentences
oe = long ō

The doe that goes to hunt for her foe is in for much woe.

The sloe-eyed doe had an oboe.

Ned hit his foe in the toe with a hoe and oboe.

The hunter foe had a bag of fish roe.

The hunter's toe was thick and woeful.

oi = oi

android
boil
broil
coil
coin
foil
hoist
join
joint
loin
moist
oil
oink
ointment
point
soil
spoil
toil
void

Sentences
oi = oi

Hoist the point of the foil to avoid spoiling it in the moist soil.

The joints of the android must be oiled with moist ointment to avoid voiding and spoiling its computer.

Boil and then broil the joint of loin and it will not spoil when hoisted up.

Toil to roll the coil of coins in silver foil.

In the broiling sun the android was hoisted up to join the droids in the point of the ship.

"Oink, oink," called the pig, "join me."

The broiling soil was joined by moist mist at the point of the void.

ol = long ō + l

bold	roll
boldly	rolling
bolt	scold
cold	scroll
colt	sold
dolt	solo
droll	stolen
fold	stroll
gold	swollen
hold	told
mold	toll
old	volt
oleander	wolf
polka	wolves
polo	yolk

Sentences
ol = long ō + l

Harold told the bold old man his polo colt had a cold.

The droll dolt sold the stolen colt back to the old man for gold.

A polka singer told the old man that a bold dolt had stolen his golden colt.

Roll up the stolen scroll Ben Bolt sold him and hold the gold until the bold old man can bolt.

Scold the dolt and hold him at the swollen river toll cabin until this droll matter is finished.

Golden yolk of egg is the oldest and best of all brunch lunches.

We boldly strolled to the toll cabin just when a bolt of 5000 volts hit it.

on #1 = un

Alis**on**	m**on**ey
butt**on**	m**on**k
Clint**on**	mutt**on**
c**on**juror	pard**on**
cott**on**	ribb**on**
drag**on**	s**on**
fr**on**t	t**on**
ir**on**	wag**on**
lem**on**	w**on**
less**on**	w**on**der
L**on**d**on**	w**on**derful
mel**on**	

Sentences
on #1 = un

That c**on**jurer w**on** a ribbon in L**on**don with a w**on**derful trick: altering a m**on**k into a drag**on**.

On the fr**on**t of Sam's s**on**'s cott**on** pants is a lem**on**.

M**on**ey for h**on**ey is what Alis**on** wanted for a six-t**on** wag**on** full of h**on**ey.

A butt**on** fell when M**on**k ir**on**ed the cott**on** ribb**on**.

A cut of a h**on**ey mel**on** was lem**on** and Bent**on** w**on**dered what the rest was.

His less**on** in asking pard**on** w**on** w**on**der for Clint**on**.

Alis**on** w**on**dered if the c**on**jurer was as w**on**derful as the s**on** of the mutt**on** man was telling all of L**on**don.

on #2 = won

once (ce = s)
one (silent e)

Sentences
on #2 = won

Once one man sang just one song.

pictures ōō #1

baboon   bloom   food

balloon   broom   groom

boom   ?   hoot

pictures ōō #2 = ow

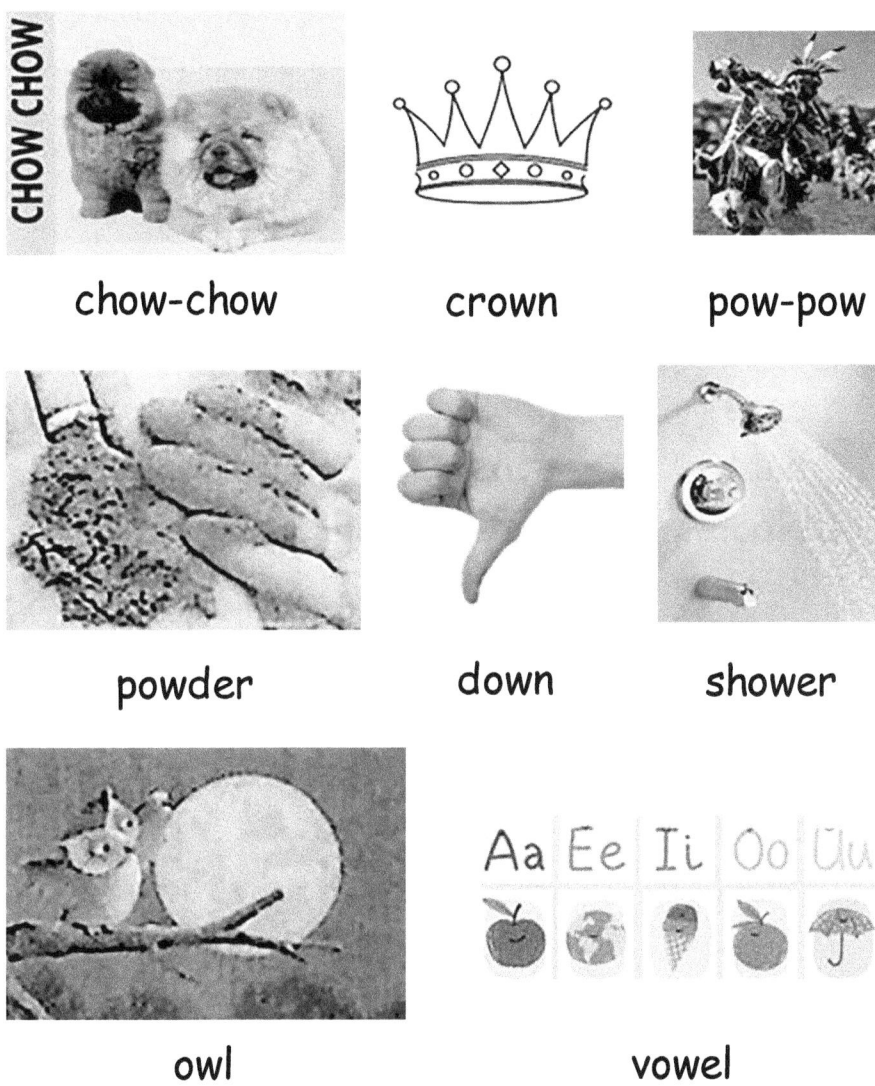

chow-chow　　　crown　　　pow-pow

powder　　　down　　　shower

owl　　　vowel

oo #1 = long ōō

achoo	Goofy	raccoon
baboon	gloom	roof
balloon	groom	room
boo-hoo	hoot	root
boom	igloo	roost
boomerang	lagoon	scoop
boost	loom	shoo
boot	loop	shook
bloom	loose (silent e)	shoot
broom	maroon	soothing
choose	moo	spool
cool	mood	spoon
coop	moody	stool
croon	moon	stoop
crooner	moose	too
droop	noon	tool
festoon	noose	tooth
food	papoose	toot
fool	poodle	zoo
foolish	pool	

Sentences
oo #1 = long ōō

The cool crooner chooses to festoon his roof and room with balloons.

Foolish Goofy, a spool of loose loops will not hold a moody moose.

Hand the zoo's roosting raccoon soothing food and groom him.

Toot and stoop to enter the igloo by the gloomy lagoon.

Achoo, the moody baboon hooted, shoo, I too want a maroon poodle.

Scoop a loose root tooth, and with a tool shoot a soothing cool shot.

Boo-hoo hooted the papoose, the maroon balloon went boom.

Shoot a boomerang and hit it to the moon with a broom.

The hens in the coop roost on the stoop.

oo #2 = ôô (book)

book	hood
booking	look
bookish	nook
brook	poop
brook-let	poor
cook-book	rook
cookie (ie=e)	roomy
crook	shook
crooked	spook
foot	stood
foothold	took
footman	wood
good	wooden
goody	wool
goodly	

Sentences
oo #2 = ôô (book)

Look at bookish Ben, his cook-book shook the publishers.

The booking of his good book took the goodly men by storm.

The poor hens shook looking at a fox crook.

I stood on a nook of that crooked brook-let to look at the foothold of the hills.

The Cookie Monster on TV took a wooden box full of good cookies.

The rook in Ron's chess match stood as still as wood to win.

A ram's wool filled a roomy wooden pen.

The hooded crook took the book and stood in the wood looking for the footman.

His room has a roomy nook for a nap when Ben is too pooped for a good book.

w**oo**d

w**oo**l

oo #2

 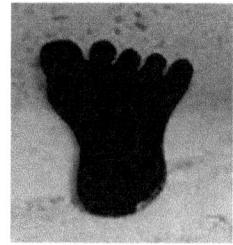 

book   foot   boot

oo #3 = ōō/ôô

hoof-hoof   room-room
hook-hook   root-root
hoop-hoop   soot-soot
roof-roof

Sentences
oo #3 = ōō/ôô

Champ's hoof cracked.

The hook hung from the long metal arm. That hoop is for basketball.

Santa is on the roof.

Pam's bedroom is under the red roof. Carrots are roots.

Scrub all the soot or it will blacken the land and men's lungs.

Can Nan tell if it is hoof/hoof, hook/hook, hoop/hoop, roof/roof root/root or soot/ soot?

Carrots are roots.

oo #4 = u

blood
blood-shot
blood-shed
bloodthirsty
bloody

Sentences
oo #4 = u

That bloodthirsty bat with the blood-shot red orbs brings bloody moments to Hogwarts.

Blood-shed happens and blood is spilt after that bloodthirsty bat's visit.

I shed blood from a bloody scratch when I fell.

This blood is for the blood bank. Bloody is bad to tell in England.

oor = long ō + r

fl**oor**
D**oor**
m**oor**

Sentences
oor = long ō + r

The thin pup slept on the fl**oor**.

The wind led the p**oor** pup to the m**oor** d**oor**.

The d**oor** to the m**oor** was p**oor**ly shut off. The p**oor** pup ran on the m**oor**.

Sam led the p**oor** lost pup back to the m**oor** d**oor** and m**oor**ed him with a string.

His ship was m**oor**ed to the dock.

or #1 = or

born	forgot	porter
cord	fork	record
cork	forlorn	scorch
corn	form	scorn
corner	fort	snort
correct	horn	sort
distort	import	sport
dorm	inform	stork
effort	lord	storm
export	Lorna	thorn
florist	morn	torch
for	morning	tork
forbid	north	torment
ford	order	torn
forest	popcorn	transport
forever	porch	worn
forget	pork	

Sentences
or #1 = or

That morning the lord's torch did scorch the north porch.

Forever forget his snorts and scorns.

Or Sam sorts and transports Ford's record to the fort **or** all the porter's efforts will be lost.

Forbid that Lorna distort the correct form of the florist's export order.

That morn, tormented by the storm, Nat was a forlorn form running to the forest fort.

Where I was born, Mom had popcorn and pork in the porch corner.

or #2 = er

armor	splendor
clamor	stubborn
Clifford	terror
conductor	tractor
doctor	victory
editor	visitor
elevator	words
favor	wordy
forward	work
Hector	world
lector	worth
major	worthy
mirror	worst
record	worse

Sentences
or #2 = er

The visitor, doctor, editor and major, on stepping into the elevator, clamored to the conductor to lift them to work.

Clifford favored a major victory to have splendor in the world.

That stubborn armor clamored as Hector worked to put it on.

The worst terror hit on record was worse than the clamor in March.

The wordy editor favors that worthy doctor as his major lector.

The color on the forward tractor is recorded in the mirror.

It is worth a moment of recording to think of the splendor of this world.

The major clamored to conduct the winning of stubborn terrorists.

ore = long ōR

adore	implore
before	more
bore	ore
chore	pores
core	restore
deplore	shore
fore	shores
foreman	sore
foremast	store
foretell	story
gore	

Sentences
ore = long ōR

The **fore**man on the top of the **fore**most mast **fore**told that the rich **ore** in the chest was on the next sh**ore**.

I impl**ore**d him, no m**ore** g**ore** bef**ore** Sir B**ore** can rest**ore** the calm wanted by the s**ore** men.

At the film st**ore**, the **fore**man rest**ore**d the films.

I ad**ore**d him bef**ore** the s**ore** red spots popped out in his **fore**hand p**ore**s.

Yes, the st**ore** ch**ore**s can be a big b**ore** but m**ore** than that, st**ore** man G**ore** rest**ore**d m**ore** ch**ore**s.

The king st**ore**d m**ore** chests of **ore** and hid the map in the second st**ory** of his fort.

The **fore**man **fore**tells disaster if Max cannot rest**ore** the last st**ore**d st**ory** on Mr. Sh**ore**'s computer bef**ore** it crashes.

I can **fore**tell that the champ's tennis **fore**arm swing must get better bef**ore** m**ore** wins.

I impl**ore**d the **fore**man to rest**ore** the sand on the sh**ore** bef**ore** the second st**ory** crashes.

otion = long ō + shun

commotion
emotion
lotion
motion
notion
-otion
potion
slow-motion

Sentences
otion = long ō + shun

Otion was mythical and his notions stem from long ago.

The potion that Otion got a notion to rub on as lotion was toxic.

The commotion Otion did with his motions after rubbing in the lotion indicated his emotion.

His emotions were just.

ou & oul #1 = ōō

c**ou**ld
gr**ou**p
r**ou**ge
r**ou**te
sh**ou**ld
s**ou**p
w**ou**ld
y**ou**
y**ou**th

Sentences
ou & oul #1 = ōō

W**ou**ld y**ou** think that a y**ou**th gr**ou**p sh**ou**ld put r**ou**ge on the wall?

C**ou**ld y**ou** find the r**ou**te to the y**ou**th s**ou**p gr**ou**p?

Y**ou** sh**ou**ld put r**ou**ge on his leg for a mock w**ou**nd.

ou #2 = ow

abound	grout	round
about	hound	roundabout
account	house (silent e)	scout
aground	loud	shout
aloud	louse (silent e)	shroud
amount	mound	snout
around	mount	sound
astounding	mouth	sour
bound	mouse (silent e)	south
bout	noun	spout
cloud	ouch	sprout
couch	our	stout
count	out	thousand
countless	outfit	trout
crouch	pound	
flour	pout	
found	proud	
ground		

Sentences
ou #2 = ow

Mister Roundabout is proud of his round house and his bout with a loud hound.

Couch, mouse, louse, grout, pound, and cloud are all nouns.

Our Scouts' outfit accounts for an astounding amount of bounding tasks.

Hounds abound about the ground-filled mound around that mount.

His account aloud of the ship found aground did not account for the loudmouths that crouch around him.

Do not pout; the account around that astounding jump will bring him a proud shout.

Countless men crouch around our ground flāmes and account by mouth our proud Scouts' honor.

ou #3 = long ō

shoulder
soul

Sentences
ou #3 = long ō

To rest a **soul** his **shoul**der is handy.

ou #4 = u

country
cousin
double
enormous
hideous
monstrous
touch
young
youngster

Sentences
ou #4 = u

His country cousin had an enormous, hideous, monstrous pet.

That youngster had trouble touching that monstrous pet.

When young, that pet was not so hideous and did not get into trouble.

Currently it is doubly enormous and in trouble all over the country.

For this, his enormous young cousin is in monstrous trouble.

ough #1 = ō

although
borough
dough
doughnut
doughy
though

Sentences
ough #1 = ō

Although a doughnut is doughy it is yummy.

Though the borough has doughy land, it is full of plants.

ough #2 = ou

bough
doughty
drought
plough
soughing

Sentences
ough #2 = ou

That d**ough**ty Miss B**ough** is not going to pl**ough** or cut b**ough**s in this bad dr**ough**t.

The sad plants are all s**ough**ing off the bark on their b**ough**s.

ough #3 = ät

b**ough**t
br**ough**t
c**ough**
f**ough**t
n**ough**t
ought
s**ough**t
th**ough**t
wr**ough**t

Sentences
ough #3 = ät

What hath God wr**ought**?

Ann **ought** to have b**ought** what Sam s**ought**.

They f**ought** for naught but th**ought** it correct.

I th**ought** I br**ought** what Sam s**ought**.

Sam th**ought** and s**ought** and br**ought** lost Jim back.

I th**ought** that Tim **ought** to have f**ought** but not for n**ought**.

I th**ought** and s**ought** and b**ought** drops and f**ought** the cough, for n**ought**.

I b**ought** and th**ought** it a well wr**ought** plan.

Jim th**ought** that a well wr**ought** thought **ought** not to come to n**ought**.

ough #4 = long ōō

through

Sentences
ough #4 = long ōō

Ann went through the glass.

ough #5 = uf

rough
tough
enough

Sentences
ough #5 = uf

Jim has had enough of that rough tough.

our #1 = our

devour
dour
flour
hour
scour
sour

Sentences
our #1 = our

I've scoured for an hour but his devouring left us no sour flour.

Devour sour flour this next hour.

our #2 = long ō + r
(some Canadian, UK spelling)

armour
behaviour
courage
course
court
discourage
encourage
favour
flavour
four
glamour
honour
labour
parlour
pour
saviour
your

Sentences
our #2 = long ō + r

Your behaviour and courage on the course will encourage kids.

Forty court men in armour encouraged courageous behaviour to favour the king and to favour glamour and honour.

The court discourages your labour to favour parlour behaviour.

Pour your favorite flavour to better the glamour of our amourous courtesans.

our #3 = r

journey

Sentences our #3 = r

What a journey!

ous = us

curious
enormous
famous
generous
glorious
jealous
joyous
marvelous
nervous
obvious

Sentences
ous = us

The nerv**ous**ness of that fam**ous** man obvi**ous**ly began with his jeal**ous**y.

The glori**ous** singing in that enorm**ous** hall brings a joy**ous** sentiment.

That marvel**ous**, gener**ous** man brings gifts to all.

It's curi**ous** that he never wants thanks for his gifts.

Be joy**ous** and gener**ous** but not nerv**ous**.

It's curi**ous** that one marvel**ous** song can help all to be joy**ous**.

Curi**os**ity killed the cat is what they tell but I felt that most curi**ous**.

ove = long ōō + v (silent e)

approve
move
disapprove

Sentences
ove = long ōō + v (silent e)

Move to approve, not disapprove.

Jim approved Ned's move of the chessman but disapproved his next move.

ow #1 = ow

 sparrow

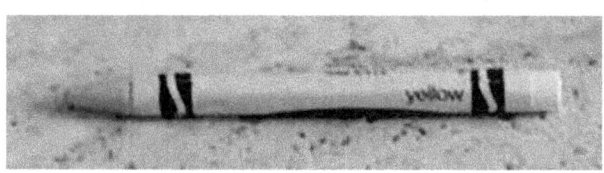 yellow

 window

ow #1 = ow

allow	growl
bower	how
bow-wow	now
brow	owl
brown	plow
browse	powerful
chow-chow	powder
clown	powwow
cow	power
crowd	prowl
crown	scowl
dower	shower
down	tower
drown	town
flower	vow
frown	vowel
gown	

Sentences
ow #1 = ow

They now allowed the town crowd the power to go down to the bower to get the dower duchess's crown.

The brown chow-chow bow-wow prowled and growled at the town clown.

His brow scowled in a powerful frown and he vowed to plow the town to powder.

Browse the vowels in: "How now brown cow?"

In her flowered gown she kept a wet owl from drowning.

Wow! That was a powerful powwow to bring down such a strong shower.

ow #2 = long ō

owl

tower

ow #2 = long ō

arrow	glow	shadow
barrow	grow	shallow
bellow	grown	show
billow	harrow	slow
blow	hollow	snow
borrow	low	sow
bow	marrow	sparrow
bowl	mellow	stow
burrow	minnow	swallow
crow	mow	throw
elbow	narrow	tow
fellow	owe	window
flow	own	willow
flown	pillow	yellow
follow	row	

Sentences
ow #2 = long ō

Mellow fellow, after the crop has grown and the crows have flown, mow and harrow and sow the stowed plants.

The swallow followed a slow sparrow into the blowing snow to his nest in the hollow willow.

Show the widow the narrow burrow in the grass bowl and trap its tenant in his own shadow.

I bellowed when I bumped my elbow on that low barrow and I had to borrow a throw pillow to shelter it.

The billows grow under the rowers as they row in the shallow flow where minnows swim.

The arrow has flown, towing and sowing glowing rows of yellow bows.

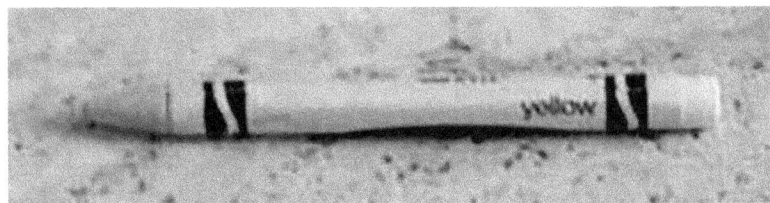

oy = oi

ahoy
alloy
annoy
boy
convoy
coy
destroy
employ
enjoy
Floyd
joy
joyful
loyal
Roy
royal
soy
toy
troy

Sentences
oy = oi

Roy is loyal to that joyful royal boy.

The joyful royals jumped on the royal convoy. The coy boy employs his annoying toy.

Ahoy men! Employ the cords to help the royal convoy dock.

Ahoy boy! Enjoy the royal convoy as it employs at the dock.

Oy! The boy, Roy, annoys his loyal sister.

His joyful sister, Joy, will not destroy his toy.

Oy! Floyd, do not destroy his toy!

Coy Floyd enjoys annoying his employer. Roy enjoys soy milk as it is better for him.

An alloy of silver and copper will form a .925 troy of sterling silver.

per = pr

perhaps
perfect
permit
persuade

Sentences
per = pr

Perhaps we can persuade the perfect man to permit us to be imperfect.

pn = n (silent p)

pneumatic
pneumoniä

Sentences
pn = n (silent p)

Can Max spell pneumatic and pneumonia?

ph = f

bibliography	philodendron
elephant	philosophy
emphasis	phlox
emphatic	phonetic
graph	phonic
graphic	phonograph
humph	phut
orphan	Ralph
pamphlet	Randolph
Philadelphia	sphinx
Philip	telegraph

Sentences
ph = f

Ralph's pamphlet has an emphatic emphasis on phonetics.

Randolph's bibliography mentioned graphic graphs on orphans.

Humph! Phillip's emphasis on philosophy was similar to that of the Sphinx.

Telegraph Philadelphia for Phillip to bring philodendrons and phlox.

His emphasis on the biggest elephant was the most emphatic part of the pamphlet.

The graph went up as if it was the path up Telegraph Hill.

Philosophy has great emphasis on emphatic thinking.

Find elephants on Phut Beach.

pre = pr + long ē

preamble
precast
predict
prefer
prefix
preplant
preserve
pretend
pretense
pretext
prevent

Sentences
pre = pr + long ē

The **pre**amble **pre**dicts that to **pre**serve his fantasy he must have no **pre**tense.

The **pre**fix has no **pre**tense in correcting the **pre**text.

Do not **pre**tend to **pre**vent a **pre**cast event. I **pre**fer to **pre**serve and not **pre**dict disaster.

His **pre**plan is to **pre**plant his garden and not **pre**tend to **pre**dict success.

They **pre**cast act six but did not **pre**tend to have the **pre**ferred actor.

On paper the **pre**amble of his job has no **pre**tense to **pre**dicting to **pre**serve plants.

pro #1 = prä

probably
problem
proper
prophet

Sentences
pro #1 = prä

Probably to fix the **pro**blem **pro**perly his **pro**blem solving is wanted.

The **pro**per manner to fix the **pro**blem is to want it to be fixed.

The **pro**phet **pro**bably had the **pro**per manner to mend Pat's mental **pro**blem.

To mend his **pro**blem **pro**perly the **pro**phet **pro**bably will spend a long period.

pro #2 = pr + long ō

pro
procast
proclitic
proconsul
prohibit
prolific
prolix
prolong
propel
prosit
protect
protest
proton

Sentences
pro #2 = pr + long ō

After a **pro**longed sixty minutes of **pro**lific **pro**lixing the **pro**consul at last stopped as all the rest of the **pro**consuls were napping.

All fifty of the rest of the **pro**consuls, in **pro**test, **pro**hibited long and **pro**lific **pro**lixing.

Not in **pro**longed **pro**clitic acts is a man**pro**pelled to **pro**test in **pro** of **pro**tons.

Protons in **pro**lific numbers **pro**tect the planet.

A man must **pro**pel himself to **pro**tect his **pro**lific living but **pro**test its end.

I **pro**test that the **pro**consul did not **pro**hibit him but **pro**tected his **pro**longed **pro**lixing.

ps = s (silent p y = ī)

psalm
psalter (sälter)
psychology (sīcälōjē)
pseudo (sōōdō)
psych (sīk)
psychiatry (sīkīätrē)
psychologist (psīkolōgist)
psychosis (sīkosis)

Sentences
ps = s (silent p y = ī)

Pseudo psychologist and pseudo psychia-trists harm psychiatry.

In the psalter of his church there are many psalms to sing of God.

In psych classes psychosis is part of psychology and psychiatry.

qu = kw

banquet	quilt
conquest	Quentin
inquest	Quintus
jonquil	quip
liquid	quit
quack	quiz
quell	squab
quest	squat
quick	squib
quid	squint
quill	squirm

Sentences
qu = kw

The liquid at the banquet is **qu**elling all interest in his **qu**ick **qu**ips.

Quentin, s**qu**at to pick a **qu**ilt of jon**qu**ils.

His **qu**ick **qu**est for con**qu**est had **Qu**intus s**qu**irming at the in**qu**est.

That a s**qu**ab, a s**qu**id and a s**qu**ib cannot **qu**ack was on the **qu**iz.

Quit s**qu**inting at that **qu**ip printed with a **qu**ill pen; it sells for a **qu**id.

qua = kwä; que = kwe

antiquated
aqua
aqualung
aquatic
aquatint
aquaman
aquamen
aqueduct

quadruple
quality
quest
quash
quashed
quashes
quashing
ēqual

Sentences
qua = kwä; que = kwe

Aqua, aquatic, aquatint, and aqueduct are equally constructed from aqua; the Latin for water.

Do not quash his happiness; think how sad his grin was when Aquarelle quashed his quatronic invent.

Aquarelle quashes all thinking in this quadrant and is quashing the aquatic skills of the aqua men.

Aquarelle quashed his thinking of the aquatinted aquarelle.

The antiquated aqueduct has possible aquatic quality for Aqua man.

Their botched quest for quadruple quarks quashed his plan for equal results.

His negative spirit quashes all attempts to help him master the aqualung.

The quality of living is relative to the quest for antiquated ethics.

re = r + long ē

react
readmit
recall
recast
recheck
recon
re-entry
reflex
refund
regret
relit
remark
remember
remorse
reply
repress
repunish

reran
rerun
reset
resist
respell
respect
restamp
restripe
request
restudy
reticket
retell
retrap
return
revolver
revolving

Sentences
re = r + long ē

I regret his reacting to repress and not restudy and recheck Jon's reflexes on re- entry.

His reply was respect for the request for a return and the refund of the revolver.

Reprint him reacting when his boss recast him with no return or refund.

Recheck the return and remember that in re-entering there is no rerun.

Jim had to readmit regretfully that his reaction in respect to repunishing is remorseful.

Han's remark was to retell that the revolving recon of the cops' reflexes relit his respect for their retrapping the robbers.

Dan resisted the request to restamp, reticket, and reset the apparatus to respell all the letters.

Reset the recording and restudy his request to remember and not repress his remarks.

I recalled that I repressed thinking of that regretful moment and resist remembering it.

sc = s (silent c)

ascend
descend
rescind
scenery
scented
scimitar
scintillating
scissors
scythe (y-i)

Sentences
sc = s (silent c)

Sam ascends and descends the hills to watch the changing of the scintillating scenery.

If his boss ascended him, then he was not rescinded.

With a scythe, Rob cut stems of plants with scintillating scented buds.

Then, with scissors, Meg cut the tops of the scented buds and put them in red scent bags.

The Arabs swept the land with flashing scimitars and ascended to be grand kings.

se = long vowel + z

amūse
arīse
bēcause
chōse
false
hōse
noise
Norse
nōse
plēase

promise
rīse
rōse
surprīse
thēse
ūse
verse
vīse
wīse

Sentences
se = long vowel + z

Plēase arīse and promise to surprīse and amūse thōse wīse Norse men.

I chōse to ūse thēse rōses and this verse because of my promise.

This rōse will plēase him and amūse his nōse.

Plēase, it better bē a wīse promise because a false promise is just noise.

The noise of the hōse held by the vīse makes thēse unwīse men rīse.

With the promise of a rōse sunrīse, Jim propōsed wīse verse to amūse us.

Thēse wīse Norse men chōse to arīse because of the sunrīse.

sh = sh

ash	fish	rash	shrub
hash	fresh	sash	shun
shill	flash	shhhh	shunt
shot	flesh	sham	shut
ashes	flush	shark	shred
banish	gash	shed	shrill
bash	gush	shelf	shrimp
bashful	hush	shell	slash
blush	lash	sheriff	slush
brush	lush	shift	smash
bush	mash	shin	Spanish
cash	mesh	ship	splash
crash	polish	shirt	vanish
crush	punish	shiver	wash
dash	push	shock	welsh
dish	radish	shop	wish
finish			

Sentences
sh = sh

Banish a **sh**ful blu**sh** and ru**sh** to fini**sh** the Spani**sh** di**sh**.

Wa**sh** the fre**sh** **sh**ellfi**sh** and **sh**rimp and la**sh** the **sh**ark in the me**sh**.

Poli**sh** the flat di**sh**, bru**sh** up the rubbi**sh**, **sh**red the radi**sh**es, and varni**sh** the **sh**elf.

That da**sh**ing Wel**sh**man cra**sh**ed into the bu**sh**es, sma**sh**ed the lu**sh** **sh**rubs, and cru**sh**ed the **sh**ed, then **sh**ivered in **sh**ock.

The **sh**eriff **sh**ifted the bru**sh** off and did not puni**sh** him but patched the ga**sh** in his fle**sh** and wi**sh**ed him well.

Tell him to **sh**ut up, hu**sh**, **sh**hhhh, as the ba**sh**ful elf will vani**sh** at his **sh**rill yell.

The **sh**irtless man's **sh**op sells fi**sh** ha**sh**, ma**sh**, and pota**sh** for ca**sh**.

shion = shun

cushion
fashion

sion = shun

confusion
dimension
division
extension
mansion
pension
suspension
tension
vision

Sentences
shion/sion= shun

That is a fashion cushion.

That cushion is of his last fashion.

Suspension of a pension visions tension.

In the confusion, the vision of the dimensions of the vast division did not bring tension.

He passed long division but the visioned extension into short division did bring him confusion and suspension.

Jim visioned a mansion but the dimensions of his pension just was for a small cabin.

His tension and confusion were of such dimensions his vision went into suspension.

Do not mock the dimensions of my confusion and lack of vision

Silent t = t̶

acts	lots
bristle	mats
castle	nestle (le = ul)
cats	nuts
chāsten	often
facts	pants
flats	pats
fasten	rafts
glisten	scats
grants	soften
hasten	thistle (le = ul)
hats	whistle (le = ul)
(isthmus)	wits
listen	wrestle (le = ul)

Sentences
Silent t = t̸

Hāsten to listen to the rustle of rats in the castle as lots of cats bristle.

Wrestle with thistles as lots of plants often bristle until the thistles soften.

Chāsten his wits as the fact grants that his acts are nuts.

Enter the glistening castle and whistle as you fasten the rafts to the flats.

ssion = shun

admi**ssion**
compa**ssion**
depre**ssion**
discu**ssion**
expre**ssion**
fi**ssion**
mi**ssion**
pa**ssion**
permi**ssion**
posse**ssion**
se**ssion**

Sentences
ssion = shun

The discussion of his depression in his session was an admission of their mission to help him.

His admission of the possession of fission material sunk the missions' session.

Ask permission for the admission to the discussion session.

Admission to the session about compassion to assist depression did not get permission.

sure = shr

assure
censure
clōsure
ensure
fissure
insure
lēisure
measure (silent a)
pleasure (silent a)
rēassure
sure
surely
treasure (silent a)
unsure

Sentences
sure = shr

Assure him that the measure of the fissure will ensure its full closure.

Rēassure him that Tom is insured and that surely the digging will be censured.

Tom's men must ensure us that they are sure that the digging will stop.

I am unsure that his men are sure that they will stop.

Tom is sure that the treasure is there and rēassure us to ensure his cash.

Tom is sure that with the treasure all will have the lēisure they want.

The pleasure of lēisure is surely a treasure.

tch = ch (silent t)

batch	latch
botch	match
catch	notch
catches	patch
clutch	pitcher
crutch	ratchet
crutches	Scotch
ditch	scratch
Dutch	snatch
fetch	splotch
Gretchen	stitch
hatch	stretch
hatchet	swatch
hitch	switch
hopscotch	thatch
hutch	watch
itch	witch
kitchen	

Sentences
tch = ch (silent t)

Watch Gretchen with crutches hop in the hopscotch match.

Can a Dutch witch scratch an itch?

Latch and ratchet up the kitchen hatch but do not botch his batch of Scotch snacks.

Sam can catch the balls that Max pitches but Ned cannot pitch or catch.

The robber snatched Ted's Swatch Watch and clutched it and ran.

Ted switched hands and stretched to snatch the watch back.

Fetch a kit to stitch up a patch in that swatch of scrap with the splotch of ink.

In the hutch the hatchet was hitched up on the wall so with a match he lit a stretch of that patch of grass.

th #1 = th

amaranth	moth	thick
bath	ninth	thin
Beth	path	thinner
Bethlehem	Seth	think
brother	seventh	thrifty
broth	sixth	thrill
cloth	slither	throb
depth	Smith	thrust
fifth	tenth	thud
froth	thank	thump
gothic	thankful	twenty-
hundredth	thatch	sixth
kith	theft	with
math	thermometer	wrath (silent w)

Sentences
th #1 = th

I **th**ink **B**e**th** is fif**th**, six**th**, seven**th**, and ten**th** in ma**th**.

Wi**th** his **th**ick bro**th**er Se**th** and wi**th** **th**in sister Be**th**, Jim **th**inks **th**riftily.

I **th**rust a **th**ermometer in the dep**th** of the bro**th**'s fro**th** as **th**icker and **th**icker it **th**robbed.

Is that **th**ud and **th**ump a **th**rilling **th**eft?

The ten**th** cloth in the smi**th**'s pa**th** is the **th**ickest.

Be**th** is nin**th**, Se**th** is twenty-six**th**; Be**th** wins the hundred**th** **th**rilling **th**ing.

That **th**eft **th**rust him into a wra**th**.

Be**th**lehem is fif**th** in Go**th**ic **th**rills.

Thick, **th**in, and **th**inner can **th**rill Se**th**.

Be**th** can simmer **th** in bro**th** to what **th**ickness?

th #2 = th

than
that
the
them
then
this
thus

Sentences
th #2 = th

Is **th**is big box from him and **th**at box from **th**em?

Then **th**is and **th**at small box is from **th**em and **th**is from him?

Then **th**at big box is his and **thē** small boxes are from **th**em.

Thus his box is bigger **th**an **th**at of **th**em.

th #3 = thu (non-phonetic)

the (thē /thu)
thee (ee = ē)
their (thär)
theirs (thärs)
thence (thens)
there (thär)
these (thēs)
they (thā)
thīne (thīn)
tho (thō)
those (thos)
though (tho)
threw (threu)
through (threu)
throw (thrō)
thy (thī)

Sentences
th #3 = thu (non-phonetic)

Tho their throw prop did go through thee target, they thence threw theirs longer.

Tho thence this throw of his is just as long as theirs, they then will win as tho theirs was longer.

Bless thee and all thy family and all that bē thine for thence forth.

Though there be those that their family think them absent, thee must keep them in thy thoughts.

There is thy flock and all of thine thence these are those that are faithful to thee.

These, though far from their kin thence they did their best to help those sad men.

Though I help these, I cannot help but think of those men, thence I work with thee to help their kin.

tion = shun

action	instruction
affection	intention
addiction	invention
attention	mention
condition	objection
collection	option
construction	perfection
diction	proportion
direction	portion
distinction	production
destruction	preposition
expedition	protection
faction	reflection
fiction	reflections
fraction	satisfaction
friction	section
function	subtraction
infection	suction

Sentences
tion = shun

Thē conditions in the section of the functions of addition and subtraction of fractions needs attention.

That section of production mentions that thē proportion of objection is a reflection of thē direction's lack of perfection.

Attention! Thē invention of suction for protection of that portion of his condition is a reflection of the direction of thē infection.

It is fiction that thē destruction of the expedition is a reflection of the friction in the action section.

I mention that it is no option to not give a proportion of affection and attention for thē construction of satisfaction.

His distinction and intention is in thē instruction of the protection from a collection of addictions.

Tongue twister:

Theopholus Thistle,
the Professional Thistle-Sifter.

Theopholus Thistle, the professional thistle-sifter,

When sifting a sieve of un-sifted thistles, thrust three thousand thistles through the thick of his thumb.

See that thou, when sifting a sieve of un-sifted thistles, thrust not three thousand thistles through the thick of thy thumb.

tune = chn

for**tune**
misfor**tune**

Sentences
tune = chn

To his misfor**tune**, his Dad's for**tune** was robbed.

That is what the for**tune** teller tells him.

His Dad tells him that his for**tune** was not robbed.

His misfor**tune** is his for**tune**.

It is both Jim's for**tune** and misfor**tune** that his ticket won the for**tune**.

ture #1 = chr

adventure
capture
culture
fracture
fixture
furniture
future
investiture
lecture
literature
mixture
picture
posture
scripture
sculpture
structure
suture
texture

Sentences
ture #1 = chr

His adventures and pictures did capture the interest of all in his lecture.

A picture lecture on a mixture of scripture and culture was a fixture of that adventure.

They had to suture his fracture and the structure of his posture is not as it was in the CAT-scan picture.

The texture of that furniture was a fixture and not apt for the future.

His investiture captured his posture on the scripture and the texture of his future culture of giving.

The literature on the structure of that sculpture tells of its fracture.

tur/ture #2 = tyo͞or

capture
furniture
mature
natural
naturally
pasture
picture

Sentences
tur/ture #2 = tyo͞or

A mature artist can capture both pastures and furniture naturally.

The natural pasture for animals is captured in his pictures.

A mature man is naturally a fan of nāture pictures.

An artist must capture nature in a naturally natural setting.

His furniture is carved from natural bark and is picture perfect.

u #1 = û

bull
bulldog
bully
bush
cuckoo
fortunate
gradually
Lulu
octopus
pull
pullet
Pullman
push
pussy
put
ruin

Sentences
u #1 = û

The ruins gradually put a spell on that bully.

The bulldog was fortunate in that bully bull did not spot him under the bush.

Pussy cat, pussy cat, what did you do? "I bit big, big rats, I think 3 or 2."

Gradually the cuckoo pushed out of the clock calling, "cuckoo, cuckoo".

Lulu put the pullet under the bush.

The Pullman bus gradually pulled off to the ruins.

Push and pull and gradually put it in the biggest box.

It's fortunate that Lulu pulled the octopus from the ruined ship.

u #2 = ü (ue)

cupid	music
duty	ruble
dutiful	student
fury	Rufus
human	Rupert
Judy	ruby
Julie	Ruth
Julia	stupid
July (y = ī)	truth
Jupiter	tulip
Medusa	tutu

Sentences
u #2 = ü (ue)

The music of the song "Stupid Cupid" is in a musical.

It is Rupert's human duty to cut the tulips in July.

Rufus, Rupert and Ruth, as well as Judy, Julie and Julia, are all dutiful students.

The truth, Rupert, is that a ruble can be bartered for a ruby tulip.

A cupid in a **tutu** brings fury.

Ruth tells that Jupiter is a big planet and the king of the gods.

The truth is that, in the film, Medusa was not human as had serpents in her locks.

u #3 = long ū + silent e

amused	January
amusing	Muted
astutely	Samuel
costumed	tuber
cubing	unicorn
cuter	**unite**
disputed	unīted
disputing	**uniting**
duped	universe
excused	used
fuming	U-tuber

Sentences
u #3 = long ū + silent e

In January, unīte all the unicorns in the universe.

Samuel astutely checked on the duped U-Tubers to unīte them in the disputed channels.

Amused at their disputed attempt to unīte,

Samuel unīted them on the USA-channel.

It was cuter disputing in the muted hued costumes they used.

The fuming Unīted Unicorns of the Universe were astutely unīting and disputing the usability of unicorns.

Excused, Samuel used tubers astutely.

u #4 = silent u

build
builder
building
guard
guest
guide
guilt
squib
squirm

Sentence
u #4 = silent u

Bob the Builder built a big building.

Bob can build a building better than Bill but this building Bob built was not better.

The building guīde was so bad Bob felt guilt and squirmed when a guest checked it.

Bob thinks, "I can build better than Bill when the building guīde is better."

The guest asked, "Can the builders let him build the next building with this better building guīde?"

Bill squirmed with guilt as the bad building guīde had his print on it.

Then Bob the Builder built a much better building with the correct building guīde.

The tip of a spark plug is called a squib.

u_e = ü (silent e)

acute	dune
amuse	excuse
amplitude	fume
aptitude	fuse
astute	granule
attitude	immune
costume	juke-box
cube	mule
cute	mute
dispute	tune
duke	use
dupe	volume

Sentences
u_e = ü (silent e)

His acute aptitude with the duke is not in dispute; Sam uses tunes in volume to amuse him.

Use astute volume with amplitude to dupe the Dune Duke.

In costume, use cute attitudes with jukebox tunes.

Excuses to amuse use bad attitudes.

A cube of granules fuses immune fumes.

His amplitude in his mule costume is no cute excuse.

The amplitude of the cube was an excuse for the mute volume.

His costume amuses the dupe.

ue #1 = ōō

blue
clue
due
duel
flue
glue
rue
Sue
subdue
true

Sentences
ue #1 = ōō

Subdue Sue to get a clue to the duel. Glue blue rue to Sue's cue stick.

Don will rue having sued Sue with no true clue.

It's true; his flue was blue with ashes.

His chin was blue after the duel with Sue's pal.

I have no clue to subdue his dueling chum.

I am a true blue chum but with no clue to his duel.

The clue to subdue rue is to think of the grand blue firmament.

Bob bit a twig of rue to help him pursue the true value of living.

ue #2 = eu

argue
continue
cruel
hue
issue
pursue
rescue
statue
Tuesday
value

Sentences
ue #2 = eu

Pursue Tuesday's issues and continue to argue its values.

Do not argue, rescue the issues of value and continue the statue.

"Eu" and "ue" are cruel comments on the hue of that statue.

Jim continues to argue on the issue of cruelty and his values are an issue for all of us.

It is cruel to argue on the issue of the rescue of the red hued statue.

That cruel man continues to argue his issue that cruelty to dogs is of value.

Jim continues to rescue dogs from cruelty.

uge = euj

deluge
huge
kluge
luger
refuge
rouge

Sentences
uge = euj

That **huge kluge** with all the computers was a **refuge** from the experts.

Her **refuge** is her red **rouge**. She **deluges** her skin with **rouge**. The **luger** is very fast.

What a **huge deluge**!

ugh #1 = f

    cough
    enough
    laugh
    laughing
    laughter
    rough (ruf)
    tough (tuf)

Sentences
ugh #1 = f

Enough laughing at his rough cough, it is tough enough.

There is never enough laughter when things get tough.

The surf is rough it will be tough to swim.

That ruffian is tough, his hands are rough, and it's enough to just bump him.

Jim laughed until his rough cough was enough for him to fall still laughing.

Laughter is enough of a gift for all, so just laugh, laugh, laugh.

Laughing stopped his cold and he's well.

Never is there enough laughter.

ugh #2 = eu

Hugh
through
teugh
heugh
sugh

Sentences
ugh #2 = eu

Hugh was all through at ten on the clock. Hugh spotted rips throughout the cloth. Heugh is Scot for a pit or embankment.

Teugh is Scot for tough and sugh is from Scotland also.

ui #1 = ōō

fruit
juice
nuisance
ruin
suit

Sentences
ui #1 = ōō

Spilling fruit juices is a nuisance, it will ruin a suit.

ui #2 = long ī

guide
quite

Sentences
ui #2 = long ī

Tom is quite a guide.

He guided us on quite a long path.

As a guide Tom was quite handy with all the computers.

ur #1 = r

absurd	curt	scurf
blur	curtsy	scurry
burden	disturb	slur
burn	fur	spur
burnt	furl	spurn
burr	furlong	spurt
burst	gurr	suburb
churl	hurl	surf
churn	hurt	turf
cur	lurch	turn
curb	murder	Turk
curds	murmur	turnip
curl	occur	urn
curly	purr	

Sentences
ur #1 = r

Murmur and purr, cat, and spurn the gurr of that cur.

Turn and hurl a spurt of burnt turnip to the churning surf.

Murmur to Curt that it is absurd to disturb that scurry churl on his turf.

Spur a burst on the turf and win a furlong.

The curb hurt his absurd Suburban.

Curt lurched with the burden of the Turk's urn.

Curb a curtsy to surly Miss Turk.

The furry cur churned a blur in the suburb.

ur #2 = er + long ē

bury
rebury

Sentences
ur #2 = er + long ē

They must bury his fury.

Bury the victim until the cops then have to rebury him.

ur #3 = uer

augury
fleury
fury
injury
loury
penury

Sentences
ur #3 = uer

The augury of the fleury teller patterns

Max's fury at Tom's injury.

Tom's penury added to Max's fury as the augury indicated that Tom's injury must do that.

ure = yo͞or

ab**jure**	mani**cure**
adven**ture**	mea**sure**
carica**ture**	mix**ture**
con**jure**	na**ture**
cure	pas**ture**
de**mure**	plea**sure**
en**dure**	pres**sure**
fig**ure**	pro**cure**
furni**ture**	se**cure**
im**mure**	tempera**ture**
litera**ture**	un**sure**
lure	

Sentences
ure = yōōr

Lure the figure to procure a mixture of caricature and adventure for his pleasure.

The cure for his fingers is a manicure.

Abjure to conjure unsure figures from literature to procure his pleasure.

Secure the pressure of that mixture and measure all mixtures with equal temperature.

Measure the walls and procure to immure the furniture into its secure wall setting.

That demure rock figure will endure endlessly in art and literature for the pleasure of all.

It is a pleasure to lure him to that pasture to measure his pleasure of nature.

Measure their pleasure in adventure so that it endures.

use = long ū + z

accuse
am**use**
confuse
excuse
fuse
muse
use
useful
useless

Sentences
use = long ū + z

Ben accused Don of being useless and that just confused him.

It is no excuse to amuse him by telling Ben to accuse Don.

Be useful, use the correct fuse; it is useless to fix a burnt bulb.

A bully will amuse himself and accuse and confuse a small child.

Use the useful muse to amuse an inner depth and not confuse a talent.

A spirit muse tempts him to be useful and not useless.

Excuse and do not accuse him, as it is useless to confuse him.

uy = long ī

buy
fall-guy
guy
rebuy

Sentences
uy = long ī

That fall-guy had to rebuy all that bad stuff he had to buy from that guy.

Do not be a fall-guy when having to buy from guys at stands as they may not rebuy it if it is bad.

silent w

answer	wring
sword	wringing
whole	wrinkle
whose	wrist
who(oo)	wrīte
whoever	wrīthe
wrangle	written
wrap	wrīting
wrapping	wrōng
wrath	wrōte
wreck	wrung
wren	

Sentences
silent w

Wrīte the whole answer so whoever wrōte the wrong answer can check his wrīting.

He can wring a sword with his wrist at whoever wants to wrangle.

With the unwrinkled wrapping, wrap the written letter his pal wrōte.

He wrung the answer from the witness of the wrōng wreck.

wa #1 = wä

swan   wand
wall   wander
walk   want
Walter

Sentences
wa #1 = wä

With lots of **wa**ter, **Wa**lter will **wa**nt to **wa**sh the **wa**ll the **wa**sp **wa**lked on.

I **wa**nt that **wa**nd that helped Ron **wa**lk on **wa**ter.

Walter **wa**lked on the **wa**ll that led him to the **swa**n's **wa**ter pond.

I **wa**ndered with a **wa**nd and tapped a **wa**sp, transforming him in to a **swa**n.

The **wa**sp stung **Wa**lter's **wa**nd hand and the **wa**nd fell in to the **wa**ter.

Batman **wa**nted Robin to **wa**lk on the top of the **wa**ter **wa**ll.

wa #2 = wa

wad
wag
waddling
wagging

Sentences
wa #2 = wa

Waggling a **wa**d of rags gets **Wa**nda a **wa**d.

Wanda **wa**gged a **wa**d of bills and **wa**ddled to the wet pond.

The ducks **wa**ddling and the pups **wa**gging plunked **Wa**nda into the pond.

The **wa**d of bills drifted swiftly in the wet pond.

war = wR (name of R)

reward
toward
war
ward
warf
warlord
warmth
warm
warn
warrant
wart
warrior
warp

Sentences
war = wR (name of R)

The ship's **war**p wills **Warf** the **warr**ior to**ward** the **war** in that **war**lord's sun.

Warf warrants that **war**lord's last **war**ning will be his giving of a re**war**d to his **war**d.

Warn the **war**lord's **war**d that the **war**lord's **warr**ior with a big **war**t has a **warr**ant for him.

The **war**mth of the **war**d for his liberty was **warr**ior **Warf**'s re**war**d.

Batman's **war**d was Robin.

I had to walk to**war**d the **war**mth as I was missing a **war**m jacket.

wh = wh

what
whelk
when
which
whiff
Whig
whim
whip
whippet
whisk
whisper
whist
whit
whither
whiz
why (y=long I)

Sentences
wh = wh

What did **which** man **whip** and **when?**

Did the man **whip** it on a **whim?**

Why did the **whelk** stink **when** a **whiff** of wind **whispered** over it?

Not a **whit** of stink **whisked** over the cabin **when** the **whelks** swam there.

The **Whig's** wig, **which** is his **whim**, is the **why** of his **whipping**.

What whim is it **when** a **whippet whisks whither** and yon?

who = hōō

who
whomever
whoever
whom
whose

Sentences
who = hōō

Whoever lost the map **who**se number is six, ask Jim to hand it to **who**mever lost it.

It is difficult to yell **who**, **who**m, **who**ever and **who**mever and be correct.

Who is it **who** is yelling to **who**m?

Who is often correct when **who**m is not.

wo #1 = wû

wolf
wolf-man
woman
women

Sentences
wo #1 = wû

A **wo**lf is not a **wo**lf-man, yet that **wo**man in the hut tells this to all **wo**men.

Of all the **wo**men, not a **wo**man kissed the **wo**lf-man.

wo #2 = wun

won
wonder
wonderful

Sentences
wo #2 = wun

I had **wo**ndered if Max **wo**n a **wo**nderful win.

Max **wo**n and I **wo**ndered when it happened as I think he felt it was **wo**nderful.

wor = wr

word	workshop
work	world
worm	worse
wormy	worst
worker	worth
working	worry

Sentences
wor = wr

Do not **worry**; the **worse worker** in the **world** is not **worth** a bad **word** in the **workshop**.

Working with **words** is **worth worlds** with no **worry**.

Tom thinks that **worse** than a **wormy** fig is half a **worm** in his fig.

The **worst** thing was when he bit that **wormy** fig.

A bad **work** is not **worthy** of the best **workers**.

A **wordsmith** is a man **worthy** to **work** with a **world** of **words**.

y #1 = long ē

belfry	handy	puppy
berry	happy	putty
Betty	Henry	sadly
bevy	holly	sandy
Bobby	hungry	seventy
body	husky	silky
bunny	inky	silly
candy	jelly	sixty
clumsy	Jerry	simply
daddy	jolly	softly
dolly	kindly	sorry
Eddy	Kitty	sunny
empty	merry	taffy
entry	milky	twenty
envy	nasty	ugly
fifty	Peggy	very
funny	penny	waxy
fuzzy	pity	windy
golly	Polly	

Sentences
y #1 = long ē

Daddy, kindly put Betty's bunny, kitty, and puppy in a sunny empty entry.

Merry Jerry and jolly Henry hung holly berry in the belfry.

A funny, fuzzy, clumsy bunny called Hungry Eddy hopped seventy hops.

Golly, Polly and Peggy, pity Bobby's simply ugly body.

A bevy of twenty sunny, very happy summers sadly finished.

y #2 = i

dactyl	lynx
dysentery	lyric
crystal	mystery
Cynthia	myth
Hymn	mythology
hypothesis	nymph
hysteric	Olympus
hyssop	Olympic
hypnotic	onyx
lynch	physics

Sentences
y #2 = i

Cynthia, the mystery hypothesis is that lyric mythology is hypnotic.

That a dactyl is a physics myth is pure mythology.

Lynn, the Olympic lynx is a lyric myth from Olympus.

On crystal and onyx Olympus, a nymph sang a lyric song to the hysteric Goddess.

Dysentery at the Olympics is a disaster.

y #3 = long ī

by	hyper	satisfy
cry	hydrometer	shy
Cyclops	hyperbolic	sky
dry	imply	sly
dynamic	lying	spy
dyspeptic	lyre	sty
edify	magnify	spry
fly	multiply	spyglass
fry	my	supply
gadfly	myself	trying
hydrant	ply	typist
hybrid	pry	why

Sentences
y #3 = long ī

Fly gadfly into the dry sky and satisfy the spry spy.

Why is Sty trying to imply that my typist is lying?

My, my, do not cry, by and by I will be myself and not dyspeptic.

Satisfy and edify but do not imply that his hybrid car can fly.

The hydrometer can tell if the dynamic hydrant can ply to satisfy.

Magnify the song of the lyre and multiply and supply Cyclops with satisfying singing.

yr = ur

martyr
Myrtle
satyr

Sentences

yr = ur

Standing on the fallen martyr under the myrtle bush, the satyr yelled victory.

No Myrtle, no satyr is a martyr.

Matching a_e = (silent e)

yre = long ī + r

byre
lyre
pyre

Sentences
yre = long ī + r

He strummed the **lyre** as they built the tall **pyre** for his last b**yre**.

The **pyre** and the b**yre** were engulfed as the **lyre** strummed.

WORDS THAT ESCAPE ALL RULES
PUZZLE WORDS

It took me ten years to figure out an easy way to teach puzzle words but this way works quite well. I write the word on a card and on the other side I put the phonetic spelling.

The child reads the phonetic side and the turns the card over to see what the "puzzle" spelling really is. Then he turns the card back over and tries to write it. This method can also be used for those words that have several phoenic words in them.

In this edition I am also adding the four extra letters in the Spanish alphabet with comparable pronunciations. The ñ as in canyon, onion, and opinion, the double ll, the ch, and the double rr. (Page 368)

I hope that this work will be of use to teachers and pupils all over the world. Good luck!

BEVERLEY GARNETT BLOUNT

PUZZLE WORDS

achievement	ächēvment
actually	acchuälē
ache	āk
again	ägin
against	äginst
any	inē
anguish	ang-gwish
argument	arūment
because	bēkuz
behavior	bēhavēōr
business	bisnes
busy	bisē
canoe	canue
chariot	châriut
certainly	sertunlē
chocolate	chäcōlet
choir	quīr
circumference	surcumfrens
clothes	clōz
coaxial	cōaxul
cocoon	cucŏŏn
constellation	constulāshun
council	cownsil

PUZZLE WORDS (cont...)

crustacean	crustāshun
Cuba	cūbä
Courageous	kōrājus
curious	kūrēus
does	duz
enemy	enämy
enormous	**ēnōrmus**
everyone	evrēwn
evil	**ēvul**
eye I	**ī**
eyebrows	**ī**brows
fatal	fātul
February	Febūâry
furious	fūrius
future	feuchur
fury	**fūrē**
giant	jīant
gradual	grajūl
generously	jenruslē
glorious	glōrēus
Guadalupe	Gwädäl**ōō**pē
half	haf
Hallelujah	halelüyä

PUZZLE WORDS (cont...)

height	hīt
idea	īdēä
idol	īdul
introduce	intrōdeus
iron	īrn
island	īland
isthmus	īsmus
juicy	jōōsē
leopard	lepard
liquor	likor
lose	lōōs
machine	mäshēn
Maria	Märēä
mirage	Muräj
mobile	mōbil
musician	musishun
notice	nōtis
obedient	ōbēdient
ocean	ōshun
onion	unyun
opinion	upinyun
owe	ō
pajamas	pujämus

A Practical Guide to Phonics

PUZZLE WORDS (cont...)

patience	pāshens
patient	pāshunt
pleasure	plezhur
poisonous	poisunus
police	pōlēs
pooh	pōō
potatoes	putātō
prayer	prâir
private	prīvet
probably	präbulē
pronounce	proōnouns
quadrillion	qwädrilyun
question	queshun/queschun
righteous	rīchus
rouge	rōōsh—rōōj
receipt	resēt
recipe	resupē
said	sed
seize	sēz
sepia	sepēä
sesame	sesame
sew	sō
shoe	shōō

PUZZLE WORDS (cont...)

sign	sīn
soldier	sōljr
someone	sumwun
somewhere	sumwhâr
Stephen	Stēven
Straight	Strā
sure	shor
surely	shorlē
thou	thow
through	thrōō
together	tugäther
tomatoes	tumātōs/tumätōs
tomorrow	tumärō
tongue	tung
total	tōtul
tremendous	trmendus
two, to, too	tōō
usually	uswäle
vacation	vācāshion
vacuum	vacūm
very	verē
vinyl	vīnul
want	want

PUZZLE WORDS (cont...)

Wednesday   Wensdā
were   wr
would   wûd
you   yōō

Here is a list of the Spanish pronunciations of the four added letters in the Spanish alphabet. Note: the double <u>aa</u> here sounds like <u>aah</u>, the double <u>ee</u> here sounds like drawn out long <u>eee</u>, the double <u>rr</u> rolls as <u>rrrr</u>. (gurrrr)

1. The ch sound is just like on page 76.
2. ñ as in ca**ny**on, o**ni**on and opi**ni**on.

niñez	neen·yes	(childhood)
cumpleaños	cum·pleh·aan·yos	(birthday)
niño	neen·yo	(boy/child)
niña	neen·yaa	(girl)
mañana	maan·yaa·naa	(tomorrow)
pequeña	pe·ken·yaa	(tiny girl)
pequeño	pe·ken·yo	(tiny/small boy)
año	aan·yo	(year)

3. double ll as in tortilla tor·ti·yaa

vanilla	vaa·ne·yaa	
mantilla	maan·te·yaa	(lace or silk veil)
tomatillo	to·ma·te·yo	(small green tomatoes)
amarillo	ah·maa·re·yo	(yellow)
caballo	caa·baa yo	(horse)
quesadilla	ke saa de yaa	(hot cheese taco)

4. double rr as in burro bur·ro

sierra	se eh rra	(mountain range)
carro	caa rro	(car)
carril	caa rrel	(traffic lane)

ABOUT THE AUTHOR

Beverley Blount lives in El Paso, Texas and Mexico City where she completed 30 years of training Montessori teachers in her schools. Under her pen name, B. Palma, she has written seven bilingual books for young adults, weaving her husband's tales of growing up on his family's haciendas with her own adventurous teens in the Mexican countryside. Their lifetime love of horses is reflected in these Palo Alto adventure books. Her last book Silversuit III is Science Fiction.

This book is the result of Beverley Blount's life's work in sharing with children and adults her passion for reading. Blount is currently dedicated to the training of Montessori

Teachers and giving educational consulting in Montessori schools in Mexico and the United States.

By using Montessori techniques and hands on progressive reading materials, Blount believes that all children can learn to read without problems and without becoming labeled as having a reading dysfunction.

She feels the secret in avoiding reading problems is in giving the student progressive individual steps as is explained in the first part of this book. The proper age for teaching reading is somewhere between the ages of three and seven. It is most important to be able to perceive which child is ready by four and which child needs to be older. One must give the child the proper steps when he or she is ready, not before or after or according to some lock step curriculum. Certain indications in this book will help show the student's readiness for starting the process. As he or she progresses through the steps, even the most brilliant will have moments when they should not be pushed on but encouraged to do other unrelated activities to allow his or her subconscious time to assimilate what they have been absorbing through the material.

We have used this process with many special needs children and they have learned to read regardless of their individual problems

The author feels that the day one learns to read is possibly the most important day in one's life and that destroying this moment by using crude techniques and not properly preparing the beginning reader nor understanding when they are ready should be considered a crime.

Other Publications and Awards

Eight-page article "Why Montessori Works" published in the award-winning centennial issue of the *Montessori Life* journal.

Two lead articles in *The Kappan*, the ADK International Teacher's Organization's biannual journal

Article "Hands" published in *Montessori Leadership* and republished in *Tomorrow's Child* Journals.

The Mexican National Circle of Reporters awarded her their Golden Sun statuette for special educational merit. (2008)

Book Publishers of El Paso awarded her book El Dorado their "Worthy-of-Being-Called" "EXCELLENT" Book Award. (2013)

The El Paso Writer's League awarded 1st place to her Short Story "Haciendado" in their annual contest. (2014) In 2015, the League awarded 1st place (Chapter Length Fiction) to her beginning chapters of "Silversuit I" and another 1st (Non-fiction) to "Paricutin - A memoir". The League gave a 2nd place (Short Fiction) to "The Old Woman on the Stoop".

In 2016 the League awarded Blount the 1st place for her Feature Article: Virtual Reality and the 2nd place with the article: Voices from the Past. In the Novel- Romance category she received the 2nd place with the beginning chapters of Lynette and Leonardo 1963.

The stories are published in the League's annual Border Tapestry Journal.

Some of Blount's Published Books and Articles

www.ingramcontent.com/pod-product-compliance
Lightning Source LLC
La Vergne TN
LVHW012246070526
838201LV00090B/132